Who's Who
in
Science and Technology

Some other books by the author

WHO'S WHO IN BRITISH HISTORY. Artists, criminals, traitors, heroes and tyrants, they're all here - three hundred of the best and the worst in the history of Britain.
ISBN 9780750281560

WHAT THEY DON'T TELL YOU ABOUT ANCIENT GREEKS.
Did you know: the Colossus of Rhodes was nearly as big as the Statue of Liberty in New York? The Ancient Greeks really were very amazing indeed.
ISBN 9780750280501

WHAT THEY DON'T TELL YOU ABOUT ANCIENT EGYPTIANS.
The curse of Tutankhamen and why bald men smeared crocodile fat on their heads.
ISBN 9780750280495

WHAT THEY DON'T TELL YOU ABOUT ROMANS IN BRITAIN.
If modern Britain was *Roman* Britain we would worship the Queen and you could have nightingales' brains for tea.
ISBN 9780750280518

WHAT THEY DON'T TELL YOU ABOUT VIKINGS.
Blood soup, drunkenness, cruelty and courage.
ISBN9780750280488

WHAT THEY DON'T TELL YOU ABOUT ANGLO-SAXONS.
Human sacrifice, bone fights, bad monks, mad monks: how England was born.
ISBN 9780750281997

WHAT THEY DON'T TELL YOU ABOUT WORLD WAR I.
Why soldiers dug trenches - and put soap in their socks.
ISBN 9780750280464

WHAT THEY DON'T TELL YOU ABOUT WORLD WAR II.
Who won the war and why men didn't have jacket pockets.
ISBN 9780750280471

Who's Who
in
Science and Technology

By Bob Fowke
(with drawings by the same)

WAYLAND

a division of Hachette Children's Books

Plea for understanding - and forgiveness

It took a genius to light the first fire, but nowadays anyone can strike a match - each generation has built on the discoveries of those who have gone before. You can't really understand how brilliant some scientists were if you don't know what was known (or not known) before their time. This book is arranged in date order and not alphabetically so as to make this clear.

Scientific knowledge has been growing like yeast in bread for thousands of years. Literally thousands of thinkers have added to the pool of knowledge over the centuries, some of them barmy, all of them brain-boxes and most of them brilliant. If you include technologists and inventors, the people who put scientific knowledge to work, that adds up to a lot of people. From all that brilliant crowd, a mere two hundred have been chosen for this book - the ones you're most likely to come across at home or in your studies. Pity the poor author who has had to do the choosing and forgive him if he's left out anyone you think should be in.

Bob Fowke

Physicists and deep thinkers

Geographers, sailors and ship designers

Engineers and architects

Airmen and designers of flying machines

How to read this book

Gods

Ancient Greeks

Astronomers

Inventors

Artists

Geologists

Madmen

Names are listed in order of date of birth. You can find which page someone's on by looking in the index starting on page 252. Names having their own entries are printed in **bold** in the index with the page number of the entry also in **bold**.

Names in **bold** in the text are also of people who have their own entry. The little number in the margin beside them shows which page you'll find them on.

Words followed by* - you can look up what they mean in the glossary starting on page 248.

Biologists

Naturalists

Geniuses

Chemists

Doctors and bacteriologists

Mathematicians

Manufacturers

5

Imhotep

God, architect and doctor

active **27th century** BC

Imhotep is the only scientist ever to become a god. He lived in ancient Egypt and is the first person, whose name we know, who can be thought of as a scientist. He was chief minister to the pharaoh Djoser who reigned from 2630-2611 BC. An astrologer, a doctor and an architect, he designed the step pyramid at Saqqarah for Djoser, which is 61 metres (200 feet) high.

It seems that Imhotep must have been a very skilful doctor. Within a hundred years of his death he was worshipped as a god of healing. By 525 BC, when the Persians conquered Egypt, he'd become a major god, son of Ptah who created the Universe. His tomb at Saqqarah was a shrine where thousands came to be cured. The Ancient Greeks thought he was the same person as their own god of healing, Asclepius.

Thales of Miletus

Very ancient Greek philosopher and scientist

around **624** *- around* **547** BC

The world is a flat disc floating in an enormous puddle of water. The Universe is alive and it breathes out water. Water itself is the fundamental stuff of the Universe. That was theory of Thales, first of the seven wise men of Ancient Greece and founder of modern scientific thought. The important thing about his theory is not what it says but the fact that he had a theory at all, a theory which had nothing to do with gods and goddesses. It was quite a good theory given the level of human knowledge at the time.

From his home in Miletus on the Mediterranean coast of what is now Turkey, Thales travelled widely in Babylon and Egypt, learning from those great earlier civilizations but taking their ideas forward. The Babylonians had worked out how to predict eclipses of the Moon two hundred years before - Thales successfully predicted an eclipse of the Sun. The Egyptians used geometry when building their pyramids - Thales was the first person (as far as we know) to see geometric lines as imaginary lines of no thickness and to work out abstract geometric principles. He also invented deductive mathematics - gradual steps leading to a definite proof.

Anaximander

'Founder of Astronomy' and first person to realise that the surface of the Earth is curved.

610-546/5 BC

If 'down' means 'towards the centre of the Earth' and 'up' means 'away from it', then Earth needs nothing to support itself. It's alone at the centre of the universe - it doesn't rest on the back of a giant tortoise or hang from the golden locks of a goddess, to name but two choices. In the time of Anaximander, most people would have agreed that the tortoise or the golden locks theories were better than the Earth-alone-in-the-universe theory which he suggested. He was ahead of his time.

Anaximander was from Miletus, now in southern Turkey, the home town of his teacher, **Thales,** the first ancient Greek philosopher. He was one of the first Ancient Greeks to introduce eastern science, such as the sundial, into Europe. His ideas seem primitive now but they were the result of hard thinking at a very early time in the history of science. He was probably the first person to realise that the surface of the Earth is curved, although he thought it looked like a cylinder rather than a sphere. He claimed that the sky forms a circle right around the Earth rather than being an upside-down bowl resting on a flat horizon.

Anaximander was also far ahead of his time in his ideas about life and people. He claimed that all life started in the sea (a popular theory nowadays) and that since every living thing has to be 'born' from parents of some sort, then the first people must have been born from sea creatures.

Pythagoras

Philosopher who believed in the magic of maths

around 580-500 BC

In 529 BC Pythagoras fled from the ruler Samos to the Greek colony of Croton, in Southern Italy. There he founded a famous school of philosophy (a word which he invented, meaning 'love of wisdom'), took to wearing long white trousers and a golden crown and became a vegetarian. He taught that our souls are reborn in other bodies after death. He also taught that numbers are the basis of the Universe and that individual numbers have mystical properties. This interest in numbers led to many important discoveries either by Pythagoras himself or by his followers. Among other things, they discovered that the square root of two, a number which multiplied by itself makes two, can never exist (you try it).

Their most famous discovery was long thought to be the Pythagorean method for working out the lengths of the sides of right-angled triangles: that the length of the longest side (the hypothenuse) multiplied by itself is equal to the other two sides multiplied by themselves and then added together. This is very useful in architecture. Nowadays it's thought likely that this method was discovered by the Ancient Egyptians many centuries earlier. Pythagoras and other early Greek philosophers travelled widely in Egypt and the Middle East.

The Pythagoreans became very powerful after Pythagoras' death. Many of their supporters were aristocrats. But the school died out within a hundred years.

Alcmaeon

The first known dissector of a human body
active 6th century BC

Alcmaeon (pronounced 'Alkmeeon') is the first person known to have cut up human bodies for scientific research and not just to kill or eat them. He was an Ancient Greek thinker who lived in Croton in Southern Italy, home to the great **Pythagoras**. Alcmaeon followed many of Pythagoras' ideas but managed to avoid some of the great man's flights of fancy.

9

12 Like **Hippocrates**, Alcmaeon believed that the body is made up of opposites such as warm-cold or sweet-bitter and he thought that good health comes when they're in balance. More accurately, he realised that the brain is the centre of human intelligence (an idea which fell out of fashion for over a thousand years, due to the writings

14 of **Aristotle**), saw the difference between veins and arteries, and described the optic nerve which takes what we see from the eyes to the brain.

Xenophanes of Colophon

An earthy Greek thinker

around **560** - *around* **478** BC

Xenophanes was a free thinker and didn't think much of the ancient Greek gods even though he was an Ancient Greek himself. He thought that the basic substance of the Universe is probably earth. He's the founder of palaeontology, the study of the remains of life in the ground. Noticing that the remains of sea shells can be found embedded in rocks high up in mountains, he suggested that the mountains were once covered by sea, perhaps in some great catastrophe in the distant past.

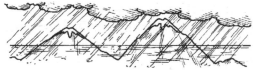

Hippocrates
"Father of Medicine"

Ancient Greek doctor

around 460 - *around* 377 BC

Asclepius, the Greek god of healing, wore a long cloak and carried a staff, around which coiled a serpent, the symbol of medicine. He cured the sick in their dreams so the sick used to sleep in his temples, which were the hospitals of the Ancient World. Hippocrates is described by the ancient Greek philosopher Plato as an Asclepiad, a member of a family of doctors and a follower of Asclepius. Little is known of him. He's said to have been small and to have been born on the island of Kos where he later founded a famous medical school.

Until very recently, it would have been safer to have been treated by Hippocrates than by most modern doctors. He believed in cleanliness, in moderation in food and drink, in clean air and in letting nature take its course whenever possible. He's also said to have discovered a medicine made from willow bark which was similar to aspirin, one of the most wonderful and safest of modern drugs. His theories were based on the idea that a healthy human body is a balanced whole.

According to Hippocrates, disease comes about when the 'humours' which make up the body are out of balance.

About sixty surviving works are said to have been written by him although most of them were probably written by later followers. This collection of books is called the *Hippocratic Collection*. Some of their sayings are still in use today, for instance: 'one's meat is another man's poison' and 'desperate diseases require desperate remedies'. The Hippocratic Oath, still taken by many medical students, wasn't written by him.

Democritus
The Laughing Philosopher

He invented atoms

around 460 - *around* 370 BC

Democritus was a wealthy Ancient Greek from Thrace, now part of Turkey. He argued that all matter is made up of tiny particles, so small that they're invisible and can't be broken up into anything smaller. This is why he called them *atomon*, meaning 'indivisible'. According to Democritus, the particles differ from each other only in size and shape. Water, for instance, is smooth, round particles which run over each other, whereas iron is jagged particles which lock together.

Democritus' theory seems very like modern atomic theories of matter, which is amazing considering how long ago he lived. His word atomon, 'atom', was used by **John Dalton** some two thousand years later. Democritus was modern in other ways too: he thought that the Milky Way was a collection of millions of stars and he believed that the ancient gods were invented by men to explain reality, not the other way round.

Aristotle

Ancient Greek who studied the world

384-322 BC

Aristotle was God - well, almost, as far as the Middle Ages were concerned. All right, the Bible was the word of God so it had to be true, but the words of Aristotle were the next best thing. This god-like reputation came about partly because so many of his books survived from ancient times into the Middle Ages. Fifty volumes (out of a total of around 150) were translated first into Arabic and then into Latin. No other scientific writer from the great civilizations of the past left even half as much.

As a young man Aristotle studied in Athens under Plato, another great Greek thinker. Then in 343/2 BC, after a period of travelling, he moved to Macedonia, to the north of Greece, to be tutor to the young Alexander the Great, son of the king of Macedonia. Thus the great thinker taught the great soldier. But Alexander grew up, and by 335 BC Aristotle was back in Athens where he opened a school, the Lyceum, in a grove sacred to

Apollo Lykaios (Apollo the Wolf) just outside Athens. It was there that he did much of his best work.

Whatever he studied, Aristotle always tried to look carefully at the evidence. (He classified about five hundred different species of animal, dissecting around fifty of them.) Unfortunately, those who came after him in the Middle Ages respected his writing but not the careful methods by which he arrived at what he wrote. His theory that the heart was the command centre of the body misled doctors for over a thousand years. As if their brains were only able to do what Aristotle thought brains did - cool the blood.

Theophrastus

Founder of botany
around 372 - *around* 287 BC

Theophrastus' real name was Tyrtamus. He was given the name Theophrastus, meaning 'divine speech', by his friend **Aristotle** because Aristotle took such pleasure in his company. They got to know each other while both were staying on Theophrastus' home island of Lesbos some time after Theophrastus' teacher, the philosopher Plato, had died.

When Aristotle in his turn died, Theophrastus took over the leadership of Aristotle's school in Athens, called the Lyceum. He wrote on many subjects, but especially on plants. Having studied more than five hundred species* and types of plant he classified them into four main groups: trees, shrubs, under-shrubs and herbs. Within

14

these groups he made further sub-groups. As well as this first ever systematic classification, he wrote about reproduction, distribution and cultivation.

Herophilus of Chalcedon
"the father of anatomy"

Ancient Greek doctor who lived on his nerves

around 335 - *around* 280 BC

Herophilus lived during a brief period when dissection (cutting up) of the human body was allowed in the ancient Greek world. He performed public dissections of up to six hundred human corpses, working in the new city of Alexandria in Egypt, founded shortly after his birth by Alexander the Great. He described his findings in at least nine books, all of them lost when the great library of Alexandria was destroyed in a civil war in AD 272.

Accounts of his work show that he examined the cavities of the brain, which he recognized as the centre of the nervous system, classified the main nerves as either carrying sensations or giving motor instructions to the muscles, and described many other organs of the body. He was also the first person to take a pulse, using a water clock to time it. Some later writers claimed that he performed vivisections (live dissections) on criminals who had been condemned to death. It's hard to see how he could have found out what human nerves do without vivisections.

Aristarchus

First person to work out that the Earth goes round the Sun

around 310-230 BC

The Earth is huge and the Sun is a little hot thing which crosses the great big sky. It's obvious - you can see it. That's what most people have thought for most of history. Around 260 BC, Aristarchus pointed out that the movements of the planets can be best explained if the Earth is seen as circling the Sun along with all the other planets, rather than the Earth being at the centre with everything circling around it. He went further and said that since the stars don't *appear* to move, they must be an incredibly long way away. It wasn't until AD 1513 that

38

Copernicus 'discovered' the same idea for himself (actually Copernicus had read about Aristarchus). Aristarchus also worked out the rough size of the Moon.

Aristarchus probably worked and studied in the great Greek city of Alexandria on the Mediterranean coast of Egypt. His ideas were so revolutionary that he was accused of being disrespectful to the Greek gods.

Pytheas

Ancient Greek who sailed north

around 300 BC, *date of death unknown*

Pytheas came from the Greek colony of Marseilles on the Mediterranean coast of what later became France. He lived during a time when ruthless Celtic warriors were spreading out across central Europe and threatened to cut vital trade routes between Marseilles and the countries of northern Europe. This may be the reason that he set out on his famous voyage of discovery.

Pytheas sailed out of the Mediterranean, through the Straits of Gibraltar and into the Atlantic Ocean. From there he travelled up the Atlantic coast of Europe and crossed over to Cornwall where he visited the Cornish tin mines. He's the first person to write about Great Britain and he explored much of the country. He calculated the distance from north Britain to Marseilles as 1,690 kilometres (1,050 miles) which is only just over one hundred kilometres out. Never having seen tides as strong as those in the Atlantic, he guessed that they were controlled by the Moon. From Britain he visited 'Thule' after sailing northwards for six days. Thule may have been either Iceland or Norway. There his way was blocked by fog, so he turned back and entered the Baltic sea.

Unfortunately, his book *On the Ocean* has been lost and we only know about his discoveries through later historians. Much of what he discovered was laughed at in his own day. Who ever heard of the summer days being longer in the north? Or tides controlled by the Moon? Nowadays, it's the very accuracy of his observations which proves that he did indeed make the journey he claimed to make.

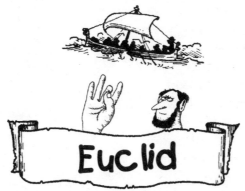

Euclid

Master mathematician

active around 300 BC

Euclid wrote the most successful book on mathematics of all time. It's called the *Elements* (originally it was in thirteen separate books). Probably no book apart from the Bible has had such a long and deep effect on human history. It was the maths textbook of the Western World for over two thousand years.

Euclid was an Ancient Greek, one of the first scholars to join a new university at Alexandria in Egypt, founded by the King Ptolemy I Soter around 300 BC, and called the Museum because it was dedicated to the 'Muses' - goddesses who ruled over the arts and sciences. The *Elements* deals mostly with geometry. It's a brilliant summary of all the work on maths and geometry done by the Ancient Greeks up to his time, and it's so elegantly written and so well thought out, that no one has been able to improve on it. It's been translated into all major languages and has gone through thousands of editions. Euclid wasn't a teacher to be trifled with - when King Ptolemy asked him if there was a shortcut to learning geometry, Euclid replied: 'There is no royal road to geometry.'

Archimedes

Naked Greek in Eureka! shock
around 287-212 BC

Archimedes was perhaps the greatest of all Ancient Greek thinkers. Among other things he worked out a very accurate value for pi, the sixteenth letter of the Greek alphabet and the symbol for the relationship between the circumference of a circle and its diameter. (Pi is 3.14159...)

He also discovered 'Archimedes principle', to do with objects floating and sinking. One day his close friend Hieron II, the ruler of Syracuse in Sicily, asked him to check if his gold crown was pure gold or gold mixed with silver - without damaging it. The solution came to Archimedes while he was in the bath (or so the story goes). He realised that the water slopping over the sides of his bath must be equal in volume to the bits of him which were under water. It's said that he rushed through the streets of Syracuse stark naked shouting: "Eureka!" meaning: 'I've found it!'. (Actually running around naked was something Ancient Greeks did a lot of, so they wouldn't have been shocked.) The rest was simple: all he had to do was to dip the metal crown in water, measure the volume of water 'displaced', then do the same thing with a lump of pure gold weighing the same as the crown. If the crown was also pure gold, both lump and crown should displace the same volume of water. They didn't. The craftsman who'd tried to cheat Hieron was executed.

In 209 BC a Roman army besieged Syracuse. It is said to have been due to Archimedes' amazing inventions, such as vast catapults and massive hooks which could

lift entire ships out of the sea, that the Syracusans held off the Romans for three years. But finally the Romans proved too strong. They forced their way into the city. The Roman commander ordered his soldiers to spare the great man, but he was killed anyway.

Ctesibius of Alexandria

Ancient Greek who invented a clock
active around 270 BC

Ctesibius was one of the founders of ancient Greek engineering. The son of a barber, he was brought up in Alexandria, on the Mediterranean coast of Egypt, one of the largest Greek cities. His very first invention was simple. He attached lead counterweights to the mirror in his father's shop. The weights were hidden in a pipe which whistled when they moved, but the mirror could be lifted up and down easily.

He is most important for discovering the elasticity of air - that air can be squashed. He designed an air-powered catapult and a water organ which used the weight of water to push compressed air through the organ pipes.

In ancient times he was famous for improving the water clock. In ancient water clocks, water dripping at a constant rate into a container raised a float with a pointer on it, so that the time could be read from where the pointer pointed on a drum. Ctesibius' improvement involved the use of gears. None of his writings have survived, and we only know about him through the writings of others.

Erasistratus

Doctor who dug deep
active around 250 BC

Erasistratus was an Ancient Greek doctor from the island of Ceos. Tradition says that he was a pupil of the great **Theophrastus**. He lived in Alexandria on the Egyptian coast where he dissected the human brain and saw that it's surface was more lumpy and folded-over than the brains of other animals. From this he guessed that surface brain area must have something to do with intelligence. He also guessed that nerves carry messages to and from the brain, although he thought nerves were hollow tubes with a liquid inside them. He came close to understanding the circulation of the blood two thousand years before **Harvey**.

Hipparchus

Ancient Greek astronomer who worked out a wobble without knowing why

around 190 - *around* 120 BC

Hipparchus was probably the greatest of all the Ancient Greek astronomers and is thought of as the founder of trigonometry*. He designed many of the instruments used in naked-eye astronomy over the following 1,700 years, working at his observatory at Bithynia on the island of Rhodes.

Using trigonometry and parallax (the apparent movement of distant objects in relation to nearer ones when the observer changes position, such as trees seen from a train window against distant hills), he calculated the distance of the Moon from the Earth with great accuracy. It was the only celestial body whose distance was known until modern times. He also calculated the length of the year to within 6.5 minutes.

Perhaps his greatest discovery was the 'precession of the equinoxes', as it's known - a slight and continuous shift of all the stars in the sky from west to east over the years. He made his discovery by comparing his own observations with those of earlier astronomers. He showed that the precession can be accounted for by a circular movement of the north pole of the starry sky, completed every 26,700 years.

Nowadays, we know that the precession of the equinoxes is caused by a wobble in the movement of the Earth itself, but Hipparchus held to the then sensible opinion that Earth is solid, doesn't move and is at the centre of the Universe. He invented a method for calculating the movement of the planets based on the idea that they revolve around the Earth rather than the Sun. This method was used right up until the time of **Copernicus**, even though **Aristarchus** had been right more than a hundred years earlier in claiming that the Sun was at the centre. Hipparchus' system was more popular because it seemed to work better.

38
17

Strabo

Ancient Greek who wrote a geography book

64/63 BC - *around* AD 24

Strabo was an ancient Greek historian and geographer. He is famous for his *Geography*, the only book of its kind to survive from the world of the ancient Romans and Greeks. It's mostly due to Strabo that we know of earlier geographers. Strabo realised that the then 'known' world covered only a small part of the total surface of the Earth. He said that unknown continents lay beyond.

Hero of Alexandria

Ancient Greek inventor of a steam engine

active around AD 62

Hero was born after the glory days of Ancient Greece were over, when Greece had been conquered by Rome. Alexandria, where he lived and worked, was a huge, bustling, mainly Greek city on the Mediterranean coast of Egypt and the second largest city in the Roman Empire. It was a magnet for scientists and philosophers.

Hero founded a school in Alexandria with one department given over to pure research. Many of his books have been lost, but enough remain to give us some idea of the range of his interests. There are designs for coin-operated machines, automatic fountains, a fire engine, a water organ and, most famously, his 'aeolipile'. The aeolipile can claim to be the world's first steam engine. A boiler containing water is mounted

above a source of heat, the water turns to steam and the steam escapes through two pipes. The boiler is on an axle and is turned by the escaping steam. The Ancient World didn't need steam engines, they had slaves to do the work instead, so no one took the trouble to develop this device. Today, the same principle, although powered by water rather than steam, is used in lawn sprinklers.

Apart from his engineering designs, Hero worked out formulas for calculating the area of triangles, cones and other geometric shapes. He also understood that air can be compressed, and from this he worked out that it must be made of small particles with empty spaces in between. With this theory he was 1500 years ahead of **Robert Boyle**.

62

Ts'ai Lun

Inventor of paper

around AD 50 - *around* 121

Ts'ai Lun worked in the imperial Chinese palace under the emperor Ho Ti of the Eastern Han dynasty in AD 89. He invented paper in 105. The tough fibres of wood bark, rags or hemp were separated by soaking them to make a pulp, the pulp was then laid out on a screen and most of the water removed by pressing. The sheet of gooey pulp was then left to dry to a nice crisp sheet of paper. Paper was much better for writing and drawing than silk, commonly used in ancient China - and a lot cheaper.

Ancient China liked to keep her inventions to herself, but the secret slowly seeped out. By AD 800 paper making was being practised in the Middle East. From there it was brought to Europe by returning crusaders. Paper mills were quite common in Europe by the fourteenth century.

Ptolemy
(Claudius Ptolemaeus)

Ancient geographer and astronomer

around AD 100 - *around* 170

Ptolemy's life is a mystery. Even his nationality is unknown: he was either an Ancient Greek or an Ancient Egyptian. Although his life was shadowy, his influence wasn't. Ptolemy's system of astronomy and geography ruled European ideas about the Earth and the heavens for most of the Middle Ages, until the 1540s when 38 **Copernicus** showed that the Earth goes round the Sun.

Ptolemy based his ideas on those of the earlier 24 **Hipparchus**. According to the Ptolemaic system, Earth is solid as a rock - a great big, unmoving sphere at the centre of the Universe. (If it's revolving, said Ptolemy, then an object thrown vertically in the air would land in a different place to where it's thrown from.) Around the Earth revolve vast crystalline spheres, one within the other, in which are fixed the moon, the planets, the distant stars and the Sun. His great book on astronomy the *Almagest* was translated into Arabic by the Arabs and then into Latin in 1175.

As well as writing on astronomy, geometry and astrology, Ptolemy wrote a Guide to Geography. He produced maps of Asia and parts of Africa. Unfortunately he believed that the Earth was 30% smaller than it actually is. Columbus accepted Ptolemy's figure as the correct size. That's why he tried to sail west from Europe to China, and why when he bumped into land on the way to China in 1492 he called it the Indies, now the West Indies.

Galen

Doctor with humour

around AD 129 - *around* 216

Galen was an ancient Greek doctor, the son of an architect. He worked for a while as chief doctor to the gladiators of Pergamum, his home town, before moving to Rome where he soon became a fashionable doctor and treated Roman Emperors.

It's amazing that someone who was wrong about so many things should have had such a huge impact. Galen wrote at least three hundred books and his writings ruled the world of medicine for 1,500 years, right down to the time of **Vesalius** in the sixteenth

43

century. Galen took most of his ideas from **Hippocrates** and other Greek thinkers but some he made up for himself. He wrote that the body was made up of four 'humours' which needed to be kept in balance: phlegm, blood, yellow bile and melancholy or black bile. Three 'spirits' flowed around it: natural spirit made by the liver, animal spirit made by the brain and vital spirit made by the heart. The weird treatments which these theories gave rise to must have caused more deaths over the years than Attila the Hun and Genghis Kahn put together.

However, Galen was a careful observer. At that time it was forbidden to dissect (cut up) human corpses so he studied animals instead. He made useful discoveries about muscles, the spinal cord and the kidneys and showed that blood flows in the arteries, and not air, as was commonly thought at that time.

But of course human organs aren't quite the same as animal organs - his idea of the human womb was based on a dog's. One of the greatest doctors of all time was basically a vet.

Al'Khwarizmi
Mohammed Ibn Musa

The man 'Algebra' is named after
around AD 780 - *around* 850

The ninth century was a time of savage Viking raids and fierce warrior kings, at least in Europe. Further east, the Muslim empire of the Arabs was more civilized.

Al'Khwarizmi was a brilliant mathematician and astronomer who lived in Baghdad, the beautiful capital of the Arab Empire, in what is now Iraq. His most famous book was *Kitab al'Jabr wa al'Muqabalah* (*The Book of Integration and Equation*). In a sense it was a sort of home-coming for maths, which had first been developed in ancient Babylonia, just down the river Euphrates some three thousand years before. Much had happened since then of course. The Ancient Greeks and the ancient Hindus of India had developed many new mathematical ideas.

Al'Khwarizmi is important not so much for his own ideas, but because he drew together the maths of the Greeks and Hindus and passed them on to Europe. In particular, he introduced the idea of zero (zero (0) is a Hindu symbol but the word itself comes from Arabic) and Hindu numerals: 1, 2, 3, 4, 5, 6, 7, 8 and 9. Around two hundred years after he wrote his book, it was translated into Latin. Our word 'algebra' derives from the book's title *Al'Jabra*, and his name Al'Khwarizmi became our word 'algorithm'. We call our modern numerals 'Arabic' rather than Indian because we learned them from him.

Avicenna
(Ibn Sina)

Persian doctor who studied the Ancient Greeks

980-1037

Avicenna was a Persian doctor and a follower of **Aristotle**, who passed on the medical wisdom of the Greeks and Romans to medieval Europe. A brilliant scholar (he memorised the entire Koran, the holy book of Islam, by the age of ten), he wrote nearly a hundred books, mostly on medicine, often quoting the theories of the ancient doctors **Hippocrates** and **Galen**. By the twelfth century his most important books had been translated into Latin and for four hundred years were standard medical textbooks in Europe.

Avicenna lived in troubled times when the mighty Islamic Empire of the Arabs was breaking up. He worked for several princes and was imprisoned several times. He died of indigestion.

Pi Sheng

Inventor of moveable type

active 11th century

Pi Sheng was a medieval Chinese alchemist. Sometime between 1041-48 he had the idea of cutting letters into a mixture of glue and clay which he then baked. He then 'wrote' his text by laying the letters on a flat iron plate which was spread with a mixture of paper ash, wax and resin. When heated and then cooled, the mixture on the paper ash, wax and resin hardened and held the type firmly in place for printing. If the plate was reheated, the paper ash, resin and wax melted again, thus releasing the type for further use.

Bacon, Roger

Marvellous medieval mind
- pity about the prison.

around 1214-1294

Roger Bacon was a brilliant medieval monk. His lectures in Paris in the 1240s on the great works of the ancient Greeks, and especially **Aristotle**, were the talk of the town.

In 1247 he returned to Oxford where he'd started his studies. Something changed in him around this time,

14

and he became fascinated by the world around him. No longer was it enough to comment on the words of others. He insisted on the importance of first hand experience and built instruments for experimenting and measuring. In his writings he described primitive ideas for telescopes, cars, motor boats and even aeroplanes. He invented magnifying glasses and described spectacles and was perhaps the first person to suggest that people could sail around the world. He was once thought to have invented gunpowder as well. None of this was typical of a medieval scholar.

Bacon was argumentative to the point of madness. He ferociously attacked all who disagreed with him. In 1257, partly due to his arrogance, he was condemned by the leader of the Franciscan Order of Friars, of which he was a member and was imprisoned for ten years. Luckily for him, he won the support of the Pope and was finally freed. It was for the Pope that he wrote his most important work, *Opus Maius* ('Great work'). This book was meant to be an encyclopaedia of all human knowledge, although that was beyond even Bacon.

But popes don't live forever. His protector died and the Church was out to silence him. *Opus Maius* wasn't published until 1733 - 439 years after his death.

Gutenberg,
Johannes Gensfleisch Zur Laden Zum

Printer to the world

around **1398-1468**

Until Gutenberg, most books in Europe were expensively hand-copied, mainly by monks. They were almost as precious as gold, and mistakes in copying were common. (Jewish copyists of the Old Testament would sometimes count all the letters as a way of checking for accuracy.) His masterpiece, the *Gutenberg Bible* (still reckoned to be one of the most beautiful books ever printed), was first printed in 1455. By 1500, less than fifty years later, up to nine million copies of more than 30,000 different titles had been printed using his techniques. This was the real start of the information age, the biggest revolution in human society since the invention of agriculture.

Gutenberg didn't invent printing, which is almost as old as civilization (the ancient Sumerians used to print or stamp characters into soft clay). He didn't even invent printing with moveable letters, or 'type' so that the letters can be reused on different books. The Chinese and Koreans were experimenting with this by the eleventh century, followed by various European inventors during the later Middle Ages. Nevertheless, his inventions were even more important, because they produced books at a price which people could afford. He developed oil-based printing inks, an efficient printing press (based on wine and paper presses) and a method of casting large numbers of letters in metal from dies (little moulds) which only had to be carved once for each letter.

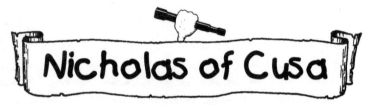

Gutenberg's father's name was *Gensfleisch*, German for 'Goose Flesh'. He preferred to use his mother's maiden name, Gutenberg. It seems that he started his experiments with printing in the 1440s but later lost control of his inventions to one of his financial backers. He might have ended his life in poverty if his home city of Mainz hadn't given him a pension.

Nicholas of Cusa

Cardinal who claimed that Earth goes round the Sun

1401-64

Nicholas was a cardinal (cardinals hold the highest rank next to the Pope) in the Roman Catholic church and a firm supporter of the Pope of his day - which may explain why some of his more way-out ideas never got him into trouble. Most of his theories weren't backed up by careful calculations or experiments. However, he had a knack for thinking up futuristic theories. And he did make one thorough investigation - of the growth of plants. He showed that they take nourishment from the air and also that air has weight.

38 Long before **Copernicus**, Nicholas claimed that the Earth is not the true centre of the Universe and that it

turns on its own axis. He claimed that there is no up nor down in space, and that the stars are other suns having their own inhabited worlds around them. In his work *De docta ignorantia* (*On Learned Ignorance*) he described the learned man as someone who is aware of how little he knows.

Vinci, Leonardo da

Artist who noted things down

1452-1519

Leonardo da Vinci was an artist, the man who painted the *Mona Lisa*. He made almost no impact on the scientific thought of his time, or on that of later ages. Hardly surprising you might say; neither did other great artists such as Manet or Turner. So why does Leonardo get included in this book when they don't?

Well, Leonardo was far more than just an artist. He was an all-rounder and an expert in many different subjects: human anatomy, mechanics, hydrology and architecture, to name but four. He cut up more than thirty human corpses to see how the body works and speculated on the circulation of the blood a hundred years before **William Harvey**. He may have come to the

55

conclusion that Earth is not the centre of the universe

38 several years before **Copernicus**. He seems not to have tried to publicise his ideas. He wrote them down in mirror writing (he was left-handed) in a series of notebooks which were never published. The notebooks contain designs for hydraulic jacks, cranes, pulleys, underwater breathing apparatus, a steam canon, a sort of helicopter, a flying machine, a parachute and a sort of military tank, all way ahead of their time. Quite a number of his designs are of frightening-looking war machines, but Leonardo himself was a vegetarian because he didn't like the idea of animals suffering.

During his life Leonardo worked as military engineer, artist and architect for some of the greatest rulers of the Renaissance. He ended his days in the beautiful chateau of Cloux provided for him by Francis I of France. Not bad for the illegitimate son of a Tuscan landowner.

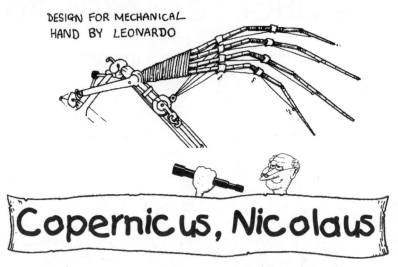

DESIGN FOR MECHANICAL HAND BY LEONARDO

Copernicus, Nicolaus

Astronomer who moved the Earth

1473-1543

In the Middle Ages people knew where they stood - on Earth. Earth was good and solid. It stood at the centre of the Universe. Around it, caught in huge 'spheres', like flies in amber, circled the Sun, the planets and the distant stars. When Copernicus said: no, the Sun is at the centre and Earth along with all the other planets moves around it, well, it was a big shock.

Copernicus was a Polish astronomer who spent some time in Italy in his twenties then returned to Poland to continue his studies of the stars. He wasn't the first person to suggest that Earth travels around the Sun. He certainly read the work of ancient Greeks such as **Aristarchus,** although he probably didn't know about the German **Nicholas of Cusa,** who claimed not only that Earth goes around the Sun, but also that the stars are other Suns with planets of their own. But it was Copernicus who backed up his theory with careful calculations. He 'proved' it - although not completely accurately, because he believed that the planets move in perfect circles, which they don't - they move in squashed circles called 'ellipses'.

Copernicus' great book *On the Revolutions of the Heavenly Spheres* was published in the year of his death. He's said to have been handed a copy as he lay on his death bed. In 1616 it was placed on the *Index of Forbidden Books** by the Catholic Church and wasn't removed until 1835.

Paré, Ambroise

Marvellously modern surgeon
1509-90

War has always been a messy business. In earlier times it was even messier than it is today. Treatment of the wounded was horrific. Shattered limbs were sawn off without anaesthetics to dull the pain, and as it was thought that gunshots were poisonous, gunshot wounds were treated with boiling oil. Blood vessels were seared with red-hot irons to close them and stop the bleeding. That's how things were in 1541, when Ambroise Paré became a barber-surgeon in the French army.

At that time and for many years to come, proper doctors didn't get their nice, smooth hands messy by cutting people open with knives. That was left to inferior barber-surgeons. Without a university education, Ambroise Paré had no chance of becoming a doctor, so the most he could hope for was to qualify as a barber. He started his career as a barber's apprentice in Paris and from there it was an easy step to the French army. There was plenty of work for barber-surgeons in the army.

Paré stopped using boiling oil. He treated wounds with soothing ointments and, instead of searing with hot irons, he tied up the larger blood vessels with ligatures. His treatments caused a lot less agony to the patients, and a lot less patients died.

His methods spread, as did his fame, even though he wrote about his discoveries in common French and not in learned Latin. He became chief surgeon to four French kings who had more use for his talents than for snooty doctors who read Latin. In addition to surgery, he pioneered the use of artificial limbs and false teeth and even fitted artificial eyes for some of his patients made from gold and silver.

Mercator, Gerardus

Engraver who projected a map
1512-94

The world is round and maps are flat. On early maps, a straight path over the surface of the Earth couldn't be drawn with a straight line because such a path isn't really straight. It follows the curve of the Earth, so really it's curved. This didn't matter to the ancient Greeks, because their maps described such a small section of the world that it might as well have been flat for all the difference it made. But the sixteenth century was different. Sixteenth century European sailors sailed all over the world in their little wooden ships and they needed maps to help them find their way about its curved surface.

Gerhard Kremer (*Gerardus Mercator* is his latinized pen name) was a skilled engraver, instrument maker and mathematician. He worked at the University of Louvain (in modern Belgium) and began drawing maps in 1534. He continued working there, apart from seven months in prison because he was a Protestant, until 1552 when he moved to Protestant Germany.

During all this time he was thinking about how to make a map which would be useful to sailors. His great map of the world, published in 1569, was a triumph. Imagine a giant tube of cardboard has been rolled round the Earth, touching the Earth at the equator. A light within the Earth shines outwards, and features on the surface of the Earth are projected on to the cardboard as shadows. Now unroll the cardboard. That's a Mercator projection. In it, all the lines of longitude are straight and they don't meet at the poles as they do in reality. This means that east-west distances are stretched out the further north or south you go, and countries like Canada look even more enormous than they actually are. But this distortion allows navigators to plot a straight compass course with a straight line.

Mercator also gave us the word 'Atlas'. A picture of Atlas, a figure from Greek mythology, holding the world on his shoulders, was on the cover of a book of his maps.

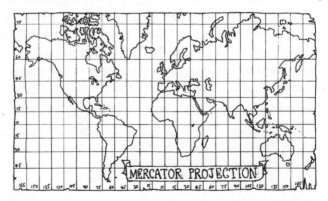

Vesalius, Andreas

Belgian doctor who cut up corpses and started a revolution

1514-64

Andreas Vesalius came from a long line of Belgian doctors. His father was a court doctor to the Holy Roman Emperor Charles V. Andreas studied at the University of Paris where he learned how to dissect (cut up) human corpses (cadavers). Dissection of human remains was frowned on, but not impossible at the time.

At that time the medical theories of the Greek-Roman doctor **Galen** still reigned supreme in Europe. But Vesalius started to have doubts. It seemed to him that Galen had based his theories on dissections of dogs, monkeys and pigs. Vesalius moved to Italy where the scientific atmosphere was freer and respect for Galen wasn't quite so important as in Paris. From 1537-42 he was professor at the medical school in Padua, and his doubts about Galen hardened into certainties. In 1543, still only twenty-eight, he published his amazing book *De humani corporis fabrica* (*On the Structure of the Human Body*). This was the first modern book of anatomy and it came out in the same year as the Polish astronomer **Copernicus** published his great work *De Revolutionibus*, knocking the Earth from its position at the centre of the Universe. 1543 was the year that started modern science.

De humani corporis fabrica was beautifully illustrated in the studio of the great artist Titian, in Venice. It shocked the old school of doctors who followed Galen. Among other things, it showed that men have the same number of ribs as women, not one less due to God having taken one out of Adam to make Eve in the Garden of Eden (as described in the book of Genesis in the Bible).

Vesalius became famous almost overnight. He was made a doctor to Charles V as his father had been. But his enemies very slowly recovered from the shock and he was accused of heresy and body-snatching. He was in danger of execution. Instead of execution however, he was sentenced to make a pilgrimage to Jerusalem. He died on the way back from that pilgrimage.

Gilbert, William

He gave us electrics
1544-1603

William Gilbert was Elizabeth I's doctor. He was fascinated by magnets and published a book on them in 1600, the first scientific book in the English language. In this book he showed that garlic doesn't destroy magnetism, then a common belief, and described for the first time how the Earth itself is an enormous magnet and that compass needles align themselves with the magnetic north and south poles. He even thought that the planets are held in their orbits by magnetism. Many of his ideas were backed up by careful experiments. **Galileo** called him the 'father of experimentation'.

50

Since the time of the Ancient Greeks it had been known that amber will attract light objects and even give off sparks if it's been rubbed first. Gilbert thought that this effect was a bit like magnetism, so he became interested in it. He found that all kinds of materials will act in the same way. We now know that they're electrical insulators and the rubbing charges them with static electricity. He coined the word 'electrics', from *elektron*, the Greek for amber, to describe substances which can be charged with static electricity.

Brahe, Tycho

Noseless Danish nobleman and the last of the naked-eye astronomers.

1546-1601

Tycho Brahe was the son of a Danish nobleman who was kidnapped as a child and brought up by a childless uncle. He was difficult and quarrelsome. When only nineteen he fought a duel and got his nose chopped off. For the rest of his life he wore a silver nose.

In 1576, Frederick II of Denmark allowed him to use the little island of Ven, near Copenhagen, to build an observatory. The observatory was beautiful and even had a water-pressure toilet - unheard of in those days. Brahe set out to correct every single astronomical record made up to that time. His measurements were incredibly accurate considering that he had to work without a telescope. They were especially useful to
51 **Kepler**.

As well as being the last great, naked-eye astronomer
50 (ten years after his death **Galileo's** telescope changed astronomy for ever), Brahe was the last great astronomer to insist that Earth is at the centre of the Universe - his idea was that all the other planets go around the Sun but the Sun itself goes around the Earth.

Napier, John

Laird who laid out logarithms

1550-1617

John Napier was a Scottish laird (lord) and a mathematician. He lived at a time when religious wars between Protestants and Catholics were at their height and he was in the thick of it. From his castle of Merchiston near Edinburgh he published a fiercely anti-Catholic book (1593), in which he begged King James VI of Scotland (soon to be James I of England as well) to root out all 'Papists, Atheists and Newtrals'. He designed war machines in case of Catholic attack. These included a gun, large mirrors for burning the enemy and an armoured chariot with gun holes to shoot out of. As it turned out, in Scotland the Protestants won hands down and there was no need for his machines.

The reason he's included in this book is that in 1594 he invented logarithms (means 'proportionate numbers'). These were tables of figures which greatly simplified multiplication and division, a huge chore for scientists until then, especially in big calculations of the type performed by astronomers. You looked up the logarithms relating to your calculation, added or subtracted them depending on whether you wanted to multiply or divide, then looked up the antilogarithm which gave you the result. Logarithms were as important for scientists in their day as early computers were to scientists in the twentieth century - they removed the donkey work.

Napier worked on his logarithms for twenty years and published the results in 1614. In 1617 he described another method of calculation, this time using ivory rods engraved with tables of numbers, known as 'Napier's bones'. 'Napier's bones' were similar to later slide rules. Both rods and logarithms were further improved after his death.

Harington, John
"saucy godson"

Poet who invented the flush toilet
1561-1612

In 1554 Sir John Harington's father and mother were imprisoned in the Tower of London with princess Elizabeth, the future Elizabeth I. The person who put them there was Elizabeth's sister, 'bloody' Queen Mary. Seven years later, in thanks for their loyalty, Elizabeth agreed to be godmother to their baby. Her 'saucy godson' grew up to be clever and a poet, but a bit of a handful. She had to banish him from her court after he translated a rude Italian poem into English for her ladies. She made him translate a long but decent Italian poem, Ariosto's *Orlando Furioso*, before she allowed him back.

His claim to fame is that he invented the flush toilet (1591) and installed one for Elizabeth in her palace at Richmond. He described his invention in a poem called *The Metamorphosis of Ajax* (Ajax stood for 'jakes', an old term for a toilet), but the language of this poem was also too rude and he was banished from court once more. Not for long, however. He was soon back in favour. In 1599 he fought for Elizabeth in Ireland and was knighted on his return.

Bacon, Francis

Clever creep and a good scientist and lawyer

1561-1626

Francis Bacon was an important person. He was a senior adviser first to Elizabeth I then to James I and became Lord Chancellor of England in 1618. Unfortunately he rose to power by sucking up to the rich and powerful and turning on whoever got in his way.

That's the down side. The up side is that, as an important person, his word counted and he supported science. It was mainly due to him that science became fashionable in England - people listened when Francis Bacon told them in his elegant Latin that the world should be studied by experiment and careful research.

14 He had no time for **Aristotle**. In fact he wrote a book, the *Novum Organon* ('New Organon') published in 1620, which answered a book on logic by Aristotle titled *Organon*. Aristotle had claimed that logical thought was the main road to scientific discovery. In Bacon's opinion, logical thought should be the servant of observation and experiment, not the other way around.

Although he supported experimental science, he himself was no experimental scientist. In fact he died because of an experiment: he caught cold while stuffing a chicken with snow so as to see the effect of cold in preserving the flesh.

Galileo Galilei

He tried out a telescope
1564-1642

Galileo, the son of an Italian musician and merchant, became a professor of mathematics in his home town of Pisa at the age of only twenty-five. He was a flashy dresser, a brilliant talker, a superb writer - and a scientific genius. He's one of the few really great scientists who are fit to rub shoulders with **Isaac Newton**. Up to 2,000 students would go to his lectures in Padua, where he did much of his greatest work.

67

He's important for his work on dynamics - the study of objects in motion, for being the first person to study the skies by telescope (he used to make his own), for inventing the scientific method (observation followed by a theory which is then tested by experiment - which he called *cimento*, meaning a 'trial'), and for using maths to describe the proofs of his theories. Not bad, even for a genius.

He first turned his telescope to the sky in 1609. Over the next two years he saw mountains on the Moon and spots on the Sun, that the Milky Way is a mass of stars, that Jupiter has moons of its own, and that Venus has 'phases' like the Moon. He published his findings in a book called *The Starry Messenger* and became world famous.

Unfortunately, all his observations tended to prove **Copernicus'** theory that the Earth goes around the Sun. This theory was unacceptable to many in the Catholic

38

Church. In 1616, to shut Galileo up, Copernicus' book was banned and his thinking was declared 'false and erroneous'. Galileo had to be careful - men had burned for less.

Then a new, friendly pope became head of the church. Galileo was given permission to write, but only in a balanced way. In 1632 he published his masterpiece *Dialogue Concerning the Two Chief World Systems*. It was in the form of a debate between a speaker mouthing Galileo's ideas and another, called *Simplicius* (!), arguing that the Sun was still at the centre of the Universe - guess who was made to look stupid? The book was about as balanced as a sledgehammer. The pope was furious. Next year Galileo was brought to trial and had to grovel. His life was spared, but he spent the rest of it under house arrest. Not that it made any difference. The scientific revolution was under way and nothing the church could do could stop it.

Kepler, Johannes

Scientist who squashed the circles of the planets
1571-1630

From the time of the Ancient Greeks, most European astronomers had thought that the stars and the planets moved in immense, revolving, perfectly round 'celestial' spheres, one within another. **Copernicus** had sown seeds of doubt about this theory when he suggested that the Sun was at the centre of the spheres rather than the Earth, but he clung on to the idea of perfectly round spheres.

To start with, Kepler, a German astronomer, favoured the traditional theory. He liked the ancient Greek idea that the perfect spheres made perfect, 'celestial' music. (He claimed that the sound of the Earth was 'mi' 'fa' 'mi'.) But in 1597 he went to work for the great Danish
45 astronomer **Tycho Brahe**, then working in Prague, and when Brahe died in 1601, Kepler inherited Brahe's papers.

Brahe's papers contained the most complete study of the skies ever undertaken until that time. On studying them, Kepler just couldn't see how the movements of the planets, as observed by Brahe, could be made to run in neat circles as required by the traditional theory. He tried circles of all sizes with every type of centre imaginable for each planet but none of them fitted with what Brahe had seen. The only movement which fitted was that the planets revolve around the Sun in ellipses (flattened circles), moving fastest when they're nearest to it. Kepler also realised that a force from the Sun is pulling them. (He thought that this force might have something to do with magnetism.) When he published his theories, in a book titled *Astronomia nova* in 1609, the music of the perfect, celestial spheres was silenced for ever.

Kepler himself had an awkward life. The son of a mercenary soldier, he caught smallpox when he was three and grew up with crippled hands and weak eyesight. In later life his mother was accused of being a witch and might have been burned if Kepler hadn't come to her defence.

By that time he was a famous scientist, who exchanged
50 letters with **Galileo**. In fact Galileo sent him one of his
telescopes, which led to Kepler's other great discoveries.
He thought of ways in which the telescope could be
improved and drew up plans for telescopes and for a
reflecting telescope. He also worked out how light is
focused and how the eye sees by focusing light on to the
retina. In fact he's thought of as the founder of the
modern subject of optics.

Lippershey, Hans

Inventor of a telescope

around 1570 - *around* 1619

Hans Lippershey was a Dutch spectacle maker. One of
his apprentices was fiddling about one day, when he
tried looking through two lenses together - and found
to his amazement that distant objects looked suddenly
much closer. Lippershey grasped the possibilities and
mounted two lenses in a tube. He sold the invention to
the Dutch Government for nine hundred florins,
although they asked for binoculars instead. The Dutch
tried to keep the invention secret, but word leaked out

through a Frenchman called Jacques Bovedere. It was
50 Bovedere who told **Galileo** about the discovery.
Galileo's first telescope started a scientific revolution.

Drebbel, Cornelis

Submarine scientist who carried a king

1572-1633

Drebbel was a Dutch inventor. As well as designing a
water supply system for his home town of Alkmaar, he
invented a thermometer using spirits of wine, a clock
which was powered by changes in atmospheric
pressure, and a process which led to the first ever really
bright scarlet dyes.

In 1604 he moved to London, possibly with his friend,
63 the inventor of the pendulum clock, **Christiaan
Huygens**. He lived there off and on for the rest of his
life. It was there that he invented his clock and where he
also designed the world's first submarine, the invention
for which he's most famous. It was a 'diving boat' sealed
against the water by its greased leather casing and
powered by oars. In 1620 it travelled the eleven

kilometres (roughly seven miles) from Westminster to Greenwich down the River Thames at an average depth of four metres. King James I is said to have gone for a short ride in it. Air was supplied down two tubes.

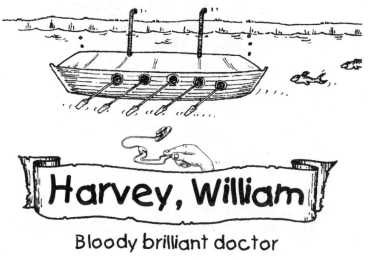

Harvey, William

Bloody brilliant doctor

1578-1657

William Harvey was born during the reign of the great Tudor queen, Elizabeth I. He was ten years old when the Spanish Armada swept up the English Channel and twenty-five when Elizabeth finally died. After Elizabeth died, he became become court doctor first to James I and then to Charles I. (He's said to have read a book while waiting for Charles at the Battle of Edgehill in 1642, at the start of the Civil War.) **Francis Bacon** was also one of his patients.

Since the time of the famous Greek doctor **Galen**, most doctors had been telling their patients that blood slurps back and forth in the veins and arteries. Harvey realised that the heart and the arteries contain one-way valves. If he tied off an artery, it bulged only on the side nearest to the heart. Being a careful scientist as well as a doctor (he dissected more than eighty species* of animal), he proved that there's no slurping, that blood flows from the heart to the arteries then back up the veins to the lungs and heart in one direction only - that it circulates. The weak point in his theory was that there was no visible link between arteries which carry blood away from the heart and the veins which carry it back. He guessed, correctly, that the links are there but are too small to see. He published his theory in a small book called *On the Motion of the Heart and Blood* (originally in Latin) in 1728.

No one attacked the great Galen in those days and other doctors fought back. Harvey was called 'The Circulator', a nasty pun because *circulator* was Latin slang for a quack doctor (a false doctor). He ignored their attacks and his theory won out in the end.

Descartes, René

A cartload of Cartesians
1596-1650

The great French philosopher and mathematician René Descartes did a lot of thinking - mostly in bed because he liked to get up late. His most famous saying is *'cogito ergo sum'* - 'I think therefore I am'. Although a Frenchman and a Roman Catholic, he spent most of his life in Protestant Holland, the most tolerant country in the world at that time.

Descartes believed that every material thing can be described by mathematics if we only knew how. His greatest gift to science is his system of 'Cartesian coordinates'. (He wrote his name in Latin as *Renatus Cartesius*, thus the adjective 'Cartesian'.) Cartesian coordinates use algebra, a type of mathematics, to describe the position of an object in space, and this was the first time that algebra and geometry were used together in this way. Developments from this system by great scientists such as **Isaac Newton** were vital in describing the movements of stars and planets.

In 1649 Descartes was invited to Stockholm by the great, but very odd, Swedish queen, Christina. Christina demanded that he visit her three times a week at five in the morning in the depths of the Swedish winter to discuss philosophy. For a late-rising Descartes this was a sentence of death. He caught pneumonia and died before winter was over.

Fermat, Pierre de

Founder of probability theory, probably

1601-65

'Fermat's last theorem' is not the last theorem which Pierre de Fermat, a French mathematician, wrote. It's the last one to be proved true, and even then, only recently. The annoying thing about Fermat is that although he was one of the most brilliant mathematicians of all time, he never published any of his work. He was the son of a leather merchant and worked for the Toulouse Parliament and he did maths in his spare time, for fun. Heaven knows what he could have done if he'd been full-time. He scribbled his ideas in the margins of books and wrote about them to friends.

Fermat's last theorem states that the equation $x^n + y^n = z^n$ can never be solved using whole numbers if n is more than 2. He scribbled the theorem in the margin of a book on the Ancient Greek mathematician Diophantus but said he didn't have room for the simple proof! The recent proof takes pages, so Fermat's must have been simpler. A proof which takes pages is hardly simple.

More importantly for science, Fermat founded
60 probability theory with **Blaise Pascal**. Probability is all about the workings of chance. They started working on it when a gambler sent them some gambling problems. Fermat also discovered 'cartesian coordinates' before
56 **Descartes** - if he'd only bothered to tell people about it.

Guericke, Otto von

He pumped air

1602-86

A vacuum is basically nothing - an area of space with nothing in it, not so much as a peanut, not even air.
14 **Aristotle** claimed that vacuums are impossible because in a vacuum, objects would travel infinitely fast, there being nothing to stop them, and infinite speed is an impossibility. Otto von Guericke proved him wrong.

While Guericke was a young man, the Thirty Years War (1618-48) was raging between the Protestants and

Catholics of Europe. Magdeburg, his home city and a Protestant stronghold, was sacked by the Catholic army of the German Emperor, Ferdinand III in 1631 and most of the city's 40,000 people were killed. Guericke and his family escaped with their lives but lost everything else. He then served as an engineer in the armies of the Protestant hero, King Gustavus Adolphus of Sweden, but finally returned to Magdeburg and became city engineer, in charge of rebuilding. In 1646, just before the end of the war, he was elected mayor.

It was about this time that he became interested in vacuums. In 1650 he built the first ever air pump and with it he sucked the air out of various containers. He showed that - in vacuums - candles won't burn, animals will die and sound won't travel. This last theory he proved by ringing a bell in a vacuum. It couldn't be heard.

In 1654, Guericke performed his most famous experiment, at Regensburg, before the Emperor (the war was now over). He pumped the air from two metal hemispheres of 35.5 cm diameter, joined together with nothing more than a greased flange. Two teams of horses were unable to pull the hemispheres apart, although they were being held together by nothing more than the air pressure around them. When the air was allowed back in to counteract the air pressure, they fell apart of their own accord.

Von Guericke went on to invent a machine for generating static electricity and to predict that comets orbit the Sun. He died at a ripe old age in Hamburg.

Pascal, Blaise

Mathematician who made the first calculator

1623-62

Blaise Pascal invented the world's first calculator when he was only nineteen, in order to help his father who'd been appointed the tax superintendent of Rouen. It worked by cog wheels of different sizes. Seven of these calculators have survived.

However, the calculator wasn't his first success and certainly not his only one, or the most important. He published his first work, a revolutionary book on the geometry of cones or conic sections, when he was just sixteen. He went on to study fluids. Pascal's law states that pressure in a fluid is the same in all directions, and this led to the hydraulic press. He also invented the syringe. With his fellow Frenchman, **Pierre de Fermat**, he started modern probability theory in order to answer questions put to them by a gambler friend.

57

Pascal was born with a deformed skull - he suffered from headaches and indigestion all his life. In 1654, he escaped death by a hair's breadth when the horses of his carriage bolted. From then on he devoted himself almost entirely to religion and spent very little time on mathematical and scientific research.

Redi, Francesco

Italian doctor who bred maggots

1626-97

For many hundreds of years it was commonly believed that certain small animals such as maggots and worms, and even quite large animals such as frogs, were born by 'spontaneous generation': that they grew directly from the substance, such as mud or rotting meat, which was their birthplace.

55 **William Harvey** had questioned 'spontaneous generation' in a book published in 1628. Redi read this book in the 1660s and set out to test spontaneous generation in a famous experiment, performed in 1688. This was perhaps the first controlled experiment in the history of biology. He placed lumps of meat in eight flasks. Half of the flasks were sealed and half he left open. He then repeated the experiment, but instead of sealing half the flasks, he covered them in thin gauze which let the air in. All the meat in all the flasks went smelly and rotten, but only the meat on which flies could land bred maggots. Redi concluded that maggots come from the eggs of flies.

Surprisingly, Redi himself still clung to the theory of spontaneous generation when it came to certain other creatures such as tape worms. It was a long time before the theory died out completely.

Boyle, Robert

He discovered 'Boyle's Law'

1627-91

Robert Boyle discovered Boyle's Law in the late 1650s. This states that the pressure of a quantity of gas varies inversely to its volume (at the same temperature) - ie. half the volume means twice the pressure and so on. He worked this out by squeezing gas in a five metre glass tube shaped like a 'J'. Mercury poured into the long end did the squeezing, and the other end was closed. Boyle realised that if gas could squeeze, that meant it was made of particles with empty space between them to squeeze into. This was a big step on the route to an atomic theory of matter. He went on to suggest some of the basic principles of chemistry: that elements* are the simplest chemicals and can't be broken down (except nowadays we know better), and that compounds are elements joined together.

Boyle was the fourteenth child of the Earl of Cork and a boy-wonder. By the age of fourteen he was studying the works of **Galileo**. He helped found the Invisible College in 1645, partly inspired by **Francis Bacon's** praise of experimentation. This grew into the Royal Society* in 1660 with the motto *nullius in verba*, meaning broadly: 'don't accept someone's word alone' - in other words: 'test scientific theories by experiment'.

50
49

Huygens, Christiaan

Developer of the pendulum clock

1629-95

The Ancient Greeks had water clocks. In the Middle Ages these were replaced by clocks powered by a slowly descending weight. Weight clocks were no more accurate than water clocks, they were just tougher and better for sticking up church towers. It wasn't until Huygens came along that a really accurate clock became available.

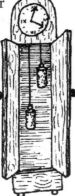

50 **Galileo** had suggested that the regular swing of a pendulum could be used to govern the timing of a clock. It was Huygens who worked out the details and made the first working 'grandfather's clock' (1657), which he presented to the Dutch authorities. This was the first really accurate clock, vital for the future of science apart from anything else.

Huygens' father, a wealthy Dutchman,
56 was a friend of **Descartes**. Perhaps it was this which made the younger Huygens into a scientist as well as an inventor. A year before he invented the pendulum clock, he discovered Titan, a moon of Saturn, using telescopic lenses ground by his own method. Two years later, he discovered the rings of Saturn (well, one of them), and in 1678 he published his *Treatise on Light*, suggesting that light travels in waves. This theory

wasn't widely accepted at the time because light can't travel round corners, unlike waves which can.

Leeuwenhoek, Anton van

Dutch pioneer who peered down a microscope

1632-1723

When still a young man, van Leeuwenhoek opened a draper's shop in his home town of Delft in Holland. Then in 1660, he was given the job of chamberlain to the sheriffs of Delft. It was the sort of job where there's very little, if anything, to do. With the income from his shop and from the 'job', he was free to follow his interests, or rather interest.

For thousands of years scientists had watched and pondered the vast movements of the stars and planets 50 in space. When **Galileo** built his first telescope in 1609, these vast bodies could be looked at more closely, but at the same time an entirely different universe also opened up - the universe of the very small and near, as opposed to the very large and far away.

Van Leeuwenhoek was by far the most important of the microscopists who took up this new challenge. He was obsessed with the very small. During his life he made more than four hundred microscope lenses, some not much larger than this full stop - • The most powerful could magnify up to three hundred times. With these lenses he uncovered many strange and wonderful creatures never before seen by the human eye. He looked at everything from ditch water to tooth scrapings to human blood. He was the first person to see protozoa (single-celled* animals), which he called 'animalcules' (1674), and most amazingly, he saw bacteria*, the smallest of all truly living things, a hundred years before they were seen again. He described his findings in 350 long, illustrated letters to the Royal Society* in London, to which he was elected a member in 1680. By the time of his death at the ripe old age of ninety, he was famous throughout Europe.

Hooke, Robert

'Discoverer' of cells*
1635-1703

Robert Hooke was the son of a poor vicar. He suffered from smallpox when young and all his life his face was pockmarked. He had to support himself through university at Oxford by waiting at table on his fellow students. Small wonder that he grew up bitter and a bit twisted. He fought with his fellow

scientists, especially with **Isaac Newton**, whom

he hounded to a nervous breakdown. (Hooke had discovered the 'inverse square law' in 1678. This helps to describe the motions of heavenly bodies and was later used by Isaac Newton in his great work on gravity and the movement of the planets. Hooke felt that Newton hadn't given him enough credit.)

Hooke was twisted but also a near genius. Among his lesser inventions are: a marine barometer to help forecast changes in the weather at sea, a telegraph system and the spirit level. Perhaps most importantly, he studied the action of springs and this led to his invention of the hairspring regulator. Hairspring regulators can be used instead of pendulums to regulate the action of clocks and watches. Without them there could have been no watches or ships' chronometers. 'Hooke's Law' can be used to describe the force which returns an extended spring to its original shape.

In 1665 he published his *Micrographia* ('Small Drawing'), a book of beautiful drawings of his observations with a microscope. From his microscopic studies of fossils he became one of the first supporters of the theory of evolution and it was while studying a cork under the microscope that he came up with the word 'cell*'. He used the word in the sense of a 'small room' to describe the empty holes in cork, but it came to be used to describe the basic units of all living things.

Newton, Isaac

'Discoverer' of gravity and all-round super genius

1642-1727

In 1665 Isaac Newton was staying on his mother's farm in Lincolnshire to avoid plague-hit London. It was there that he saw an apple fall from a tree and wondered if the force which pulled the apple to the ground was the same force which held the Moon in orbit round the Earth. Until that time, heaven and Earth were thought to be quite different and to be ruled by different laws. It was a stroke of genius to realise that the same laws might apply to both. His theory of Universal Gravitation is called universal because it applies both to objects as small as apples and to objects as large as the Sun.

Newton was already on the way to inventing calculus, a mathematical technique invented independently at the same time by Leibniz over in Germany. He used calculus to develop his theory and worked out the distance of the Moon from Earth. Unfortunately his answer was different to what was known to be the correct figure. He stopped working on Universal Gravitation for the next fifteen years.

Instead he turned his attention to the nature of light. He allowed a ray of light to shine through a chink into a darkened room so that it passed through a prism* and on to a screen. Lo and behold, the light was bent, or 'refracted', by the prism, and divided into the colours of the rainbow. He went on to shine light through two reversed prisms. The light was split into colours by the first and recombined into white light by the second. Thus he proved that white light is a mixture of the colours of the rainbow. He went on to suggest that light is a stream of tiny particles.

Newton now knew why the telescopes of that time gave a blurred image. Each object seemed to have its own blurred halo of rainbow colours and Newton could now see that the lenses acted a bit like prisms. He built the first reflecting telescope. Light was focused by bouncing off the surface of a curved mirror. It didn't pass through glass so there were no rainbows.

That was in 1668. Newton became a professor of mathematics at Cambridge the following year and a member of the Royal Society* six years later. So he was already well-known and respected when, in 1684, Christopher Wren, the president of the Society, offered a prize to whoever could solve the problem of the laws governing the movement of the planets and stars.

73 **Edmond Halley**, a fellow member, took the problem to Newton at Cambridge, only to be told that Newton already knew the answer. When Halley asked how, Newton replied with the famous words: 'why, I have calculated it.' It was fifteen years since he'd seen the apple fall from the tree.

Halley helped Newton to publish *Philosophiae Naturalis Principia Mathematica* (*Principia* for short), perhaps the greatest scientific work of all time. It described the fundamental laws governing movement, known as the laws of motion and used those laws to explain the movement of the planets. The theory of Universal Gravitation was at last fully explained. It reigned
212 supreme until **Albert Einstein** developed the Theory of Relativity more than two hundred years later.

Newton had been a strange child. He liked to make odd devices such as sundials and water clocks. At school he was a mediocre student and only made an effort with his school work so as to do better than the school bully. Even at University he wasn't very brilliant. He never married and was incredibly absent minded. In 1687 he was elected to parliament, but only spoke once - to ask for a window to be closed because of the draught. No scientist has been so famous in his own lifetime. He stands like a giant at the end of the scientific revolution which
50
38 started with **Galileo** and **Copernicus**.

Leibniz, Gottfried Wilhelm

German mathematician who calculated calculus

1646-1716

Gottfried Leibniz was more of a philosopher and a diplomat than he was a mathematician. He's included in this book because he invented 'calculus', a method of calculation based on dividing something which is continuously changing into tiny, tiny bits. It's useful, among many other things, for defining the speed that a planet travels through space. This is why it was also invented by **Isaac Newton**. Unfortunately, both men invented the calculus independently at roughly the same time. Each accused the other of copying. The quarrel was bitter. Nowadays mathematicians tend to find Leibniz's methods more useful.

Leibniz was the son of a German professor of philosophy. He taught himself Latin when he was only eight. In mathematics, as well as calculus, he was the first person to see the importance of the binary system, now used by all computers, and he invented a calculating machine which could multiply and divide as well as add and subtract - an improvement on the machine of **Blaise Pascal**.

But by trying to cover all subjects, Leibniz perhaps spread himself too thinly. His attempt to prove that we live in the best of all possible worlds (with the emphasis on *possible*) was ridiculed by the French writer Voltaire in a famous book titled *Candide*. Leibniz suffered from gout towards the end of his life and died unmarried, like his old enemy Newton.

Papin, Denis

He let off steam
1647- *around* 1712

No one person 'invented' the steam engine, but Denis Papin probably did more of the inventing than anyone else. He was a French doctor who got his medical degree in 1669, but whose interest in science soon overtook his interest in medicine. After taking his degree he went to work as assistant to **Christiaan Huygens**, the inventor of the pendulum clock. In 1675 he moved to London and worked as assistant to **Robert Boyle**.

Fired by Boyle's work on the nature of gases, in 1679 Papin built his 'steam digester'. This remarkable invention was in fact the world's first pressure cooker, a sealed container where the pressure of steam raised the boiling point of the water inside it. He also invented a safety valve so it didn't blow up. By 1680, Papin had been elected a member of the Royal Society* on the strength of his digester - and had cooked a meal for his esteemed fellow members. He also cooked one for King Charles II. Perhaps one of the grandest meals ever cooked in a pressure cooker.

Papin noticed that steam pressure tended to lift the lid of his digester. This gave him the idea of using steam to move a piston in a cylinder. He had now invented a pressurised cylinder, a safety valve and a piston, the three most basic parts of a steam engine. Papin was a Protestant, and France under Catholic Louis XIV was too dangerous for him to go back to. He moved to Germany where among other inventions and discoveries he built a paddle boat to show how steam might power a ship. He is said to have travelled down the Rhine in it, using his family to turn the paddles. Unfortunately, Papin failed to profit from his work. He died in poverty in England.

Savery, Thomas

He built the first working steam pump

around **1650-1715**

Thomas Savery was a Devonshire man and a military engineer. He invented a machine for polishing glass, a paddle wheel for ships becalmed at sea and a device for measuring the distance travelled by ships at sea. But the invention which made him famous was his steam pump, which he patented* in 1698.

Savery's steam pump, designed to pump water from mines, was called 'The Miner's Friend'. Water was heated into steam in a boiler. A spray of cold water turned the steam back into water in a condensing chamber, creating a vacuum. The vacuum sucked water a little way up a pipe which was then pushed away by the pressure of more steam.

Versions of his steam pump were operated in several mines and were also used to pump water to large buildings. However it was never very effective. This was because it used pressurised steam and it was very difficult to build with the technology of the time. Finally Savery went into partnership with **Thomas Newcomen** and Newcomen's improved design, which had no need of pressurised steam, was far more successful.

Halley, Edmond
"the Southern Tycho"

Comet calculator
1656-1742

Comets are the cowboys of the starry skies. For thousands of years their behaviour seemed completely mad. They circle the Sun like planets, but they sail much further out, in immense, stretched-out orbits. Those which fly furthest can take up to ten thousand years to complete a single, lonely circuit. None of this was known before Halley came along.

Edmond Halley made his reputation as an astronomer in 1678, when he published a star catalogue of the southern skies, having spent a year with his telescope on the remote island of St Helena in the Atlantic (where the Emperor Napoleon was later exiled). He was hailed
45 as 'The Southern Tycho', after **Tycho Brahe**, and became a member of the Royal Society*.

In 1684 two things happened: Halley's father was
67 murdered and Halley visited **Isaac Newton**. He immediately realised the importance of Newton's work and used some of the fortune which he inherited from his father to publish Newton's great work on gravitation and the movement of heavenly bodies, the *Principia*, published in 1687. Halley and Newton became friends and Halley decided to use Newton's laws to explain the behaviour of comets, which hadn't been included in Newton's calculations. He investigated records of comet sightings going back to 1337 and

realised that three historic sightings, in 1531, 1607 and 1682 were so similar that they must be of the same comet. This comet is now called Halley's Comet in his honour. It appears every seventy-six years and is depicted in the Bayeaux Tapestry of the Norman conquest of England in 1066. With Newton's help Halley showed how comets follow their stretched-out orbits around the Sun. He published his findings in 1705 in a book titled *A Synopsis of the Astronomy of Comets*.

As well as his work as an astronomer, Halley produced the world's first metereological chart, of winds in the Atlantic, and a magnetic chart of the Atlantic. He became Astronomer Royal and died at the grand old age of eighty-six - sixteen years before his comet was due to reappear.

Newcomen, Thomas

Inventor of an early steam engine

1663-1729

The first steam engines weren't powered by steam, at least not directly. They were powered by the weight of air. Newcomen, who was a Cornish ironmonger or blacksmith, started work on his design for a steam engine some time before 1698. It was much better than an earlier device, designed by **Thomas Savery**, to pump water from Cornish tin mines. Savery's engine had used high pressure steam to force the piston along the cylinder. Unfortunately, it was almost impossible to build a cylinder which didn't leak some of the high-

72

pressure steam and Savery's engine was difficult to build and was very inefficient.

Newcomen's Atmospheric Steam Engine of 1712 didn't need steam at high pressures. The steam flowed into the cylinder at normal air pressure and then cooled with a jet of cold water so that it condensed back into water. Water takes up much less space than steam, so this created a vacuum. Atmospheric pressure could now push the piston into the cylinder since there was nothing in the cylinder to resist it. Thus it was air that did the work.

Unfortunately, Savery's patent* was written in such a way that it included pretty well any possible steam engine that might be invented at the time. He had steam engines sewn up. Newcomen was obliged to go into partnership with him. The partnership was successful. Their (really Newcomen's) machines were mainly used to pump mines and raise water for water wheels. They were widely used until **James Watt** built steam engines which were even more efficient later in the century.

94

Tull, Jethro

He drilled for seed

1674-1741

Jethro Tull designed a machine for sowing seed in straight rows. Straight rows meant that it was possible to hoe up most of the weeds which grew between them and the machine made them quicker to sow. It was a big advance on previous methods which tended to involve scattering or hand 'drilling' the seed. He was a lawyer from Basildon in Berkshire who had hoped to take up a career in politics, before poor health put a stop to his ambitions. Instead, for ten years from 1699, he farmed land belonging to his father.

Tull's machine was pulled by a horse. It had a hopper for holding the seed, a box for delivering it and a harrow and plough for digging the 'drill' (the furrow where the seed was sown) and for covering the seed with soil. He claimed that the basic mechanism was inspired by the sound board of a church organ. Between 1731-34 he published his ideas on agriculture in a book titled *The New Horse Houghing Husbandry: Or an Essay on the Principles of Tillage and Vegetation.*

Darby, Abraham

Manufacturer of cast iron things

around 1678-1717

Abraham Darby opened a brass factory in Bristol in 1698. He then had the idea that it might be possible to make cheaper pots and pans out of iron instead of brass. After experimenting with various methods of casting iron, he eventually hit on a brand new method using sand, which he patented in 1708. Before long his strong, cheap pans were being sold all over Britain.

In 1709 he moved to the Midlands, to Coalbrookdale in Shropshire where he leased an old furnace. This, more than anywhere else, is where the Industrial Revolution really began. At Coalbrookdale he developed a method of smelting iron ore using coke as the fuel, which was later improved on by his son, also called Abraham Darby. Coke is produced by heating coal at high temperatures, sealed from the air so it can't burn and it's a more reliable fuel than coal or charcoal, which were all anyone had thought of using up to then. Now good-quality cast iron was plentifully available for the first time - iron which was vital for building the new steam engines. The Darbys' cast iron helped Britain to become the first country in the world to industrialise.

Fahrenheit, Daniel Gabriel

Dutchman who made a thermometer
1686-1736

Running up the centre of most thermometers is a thin thread of silvery metal in a hollow glass tube. As the metal expands or contracts with heat or cold, the temperature is read off a scale of numbers alongside it. The silvery metal is liquid mercury and the mercury thermometer was invented by Daniel Fahrenheit.

Fahrenheit made his first thermometer in 1709, using alcohol rather than mercury. However, the problem with alcohol is that it boils at a low temperature, much lower than water, so alcohol thermometers are useless for measuring anything really hot. Mercury on the other hand, is unlikely to boil in everyday situations unless you live on Venus.

Fahrenheit wanted 0° on his scale to stand for the lowest possible temperature so that there wouldn't be any need for minus numbers. So he made 0°F the temperature at which salty water freezes into ice, 32°F then became the normal freezing point of unsalty water and 212°F the boiling point of water - because it's exactly 180° above 32°. Nowadays the Fahrenheit scale is less widely used than centigrade, invented by **Anders Celsius**, but is still common in the USA and Great Britain.

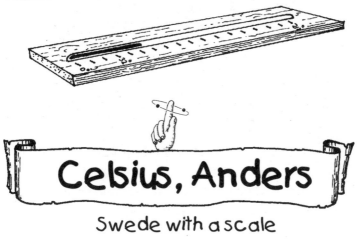

Celsius, Anders

Swede with a scale

1701-44

Anders Celsius was a Swedish astronomer. In 1742 he suggested that temperature should be measured on a fixed scale: 0° would be the temperature at which water boils and 100° would be temperature at which it freezes. A year later this was changed round so that 0° became the temperature at which water freezes and 100° the temperature at which it boils. The Celsius scale is often called Centigrade, a hundred steps, because there are a hundred degrees between 0° and 100°: *centum* is Latin for 100 and *gradus* is Latin for a step. It's now the most common of all scales for measuring temperature.

Franklin, Benjamin

He captured lightning
1706-90

Benjamin Franklin, the tenth son of a Boston soap and candle maker, was one of the founding fathers of the United States. He helped write the Declaration of Independence and the American Constitution. He was also a great inventor and scientist. He invented bifocal glasses and the lightning conductor and designed a new type of stove. As a scientist he investigated electricity.

The Leyden jar was a glass jar lined with metal with a rod stuck into it through a cork stopper. It was invented at the University of Leiden in Holland in 1745. Static electricity, produced by rubbing, could be conducted down the rod and stored in the jar. If the charged jar was held near a metal object, a spark would fly between them. Franklin had his own Leyden jar. He started to wonder if lightning might not be a giant spark and that the sky behaved like a giant Leyden jar, so to speak. At that time nobody knew much about electricity.

In 1752, to prove his theory, he flew a kite in a thunder storm. A pointed wire hung from the kite and a silk thread ran from the wire back to a metal key. Franklin then placed his hand near the key and there was a spark. He then went on to charge a Leyden jar from the same key. This was clear proof that lightning was electricity. (Actually the experiment was first carried out, and more safely, in France, although based on Franklin's idea. He himself was lucky to live: two men who copied him died of electric shocks.)

Franklin thought of electricity as a fluid that flows from one thing to another if there's too much of it in one place and not enough in the other. Where there was too much he said it was positive and where there wasn't enough he said it was negative. Unfortunately he got them the wrong way round. We now know that electrons flow from negative to positive. However, what is known as 'conventional current' still flows from positive to negative.

Linnaeus, Carolus
(Carl von Linné)

Swede who called us names
1707-78

How do you look someone up in the telephone directory if they haven't got a name? It may not matter if you both live in a little village and you know everyone anyway, but it does matter if you live in a huge city. Names are important.

The city of life is vast beyond imagining. There are countless thousands, if not millions, of species* of living things in the world, and far more once lived but are now extinct. It was vital for the development of biology (the study of living things) that there should be a sensible way of naming them.

Carolus Linnaeus (a Latin form of Carl von Linné) was a Swedish doctor. He travelled to Lapland for the University in 1732, where he discovered a hundred new species of plants. He then made journeys to England and the mainland of Europe. Four years later, his great work *Systema Natura* was published. It had only seven large pages, but those pages laid the foundations for the modern system of categorising living things. His system developed from his studies of the physical differences of types of male and female plants. (It was Linnaeus who first used the symbols ♂ and ♀ to mean male and female.) In *Systema Naturae* he grouped species of plants and animals into genera (plural of genus) according to the characteristics they had in common. Each type of plant and animal was given two Latin names, one for its species and one for the *genus* to which the species belonged. He then went on to group the *genera* (plural of *genus*) into 'classes' and the classes into 'orders'.

By the tenth edition *Systema Naturae* was 2,500 pages long. If you classify things in this way, it becomes obvious that species are related to each other - and from that, that they may have evolved from each other. Modern versions of Linnaeus' system are based on real, evolutionary relationships, not just on similarities of appearance. However, Linnaeus himself never believed in evolution. He thought that all creatures were created as they are today at the creation of the world.

Trésaguet, Pierre-Marie-Jérôme

French road builder who sorted out a surface
1716-96

In the early eighteenth century the roads of Europe were appalling. Travel was more of a punishment than a pleasure. Trésaguet became Inspector General of the School of the *Corps des Ponts et Chaussées* (Agency of Bridges and Highways) in Paris in 1775. This was the first roads agency in Europe since the time of the Roman Empire. He developed a new method of road building. The road surface was dug out to a depth of about 25 cm and flat stones were hammered into it - on edge, so that water could drain between them. A surface of small stones was then poured on top and then the whole thing was rolled smooth.

Trésaguet built a major road from Paris to the Spanish/French border with his new technique. It was then copied and improved on by **Thomas Telford** in England, but was finally overtaken by macadam, invented by **John Loudon McAdam** in the early nineteenth century, which was better and cheaper.

115
114

Hargreaves, James

Inventor of a spinning machine
around 1720-78

James Hargreaves was a weaver from Blackburn in Lancashire. Around 1764 he invented a spinning 'jenny'. No one knows why he called his machine a 'jenny' although one tradition says that he didn't actually invent the machine, but merely improved on the invention of a Mr Highes, and that the machine was named after Highes' daughter Jane.

Using Hargreaves' 'spinning jenny', one worker could produce as much thread or yarn as eight ordinary hand-workers. In 1766 he sold some machines outside the family to make extra cash. From that time, local hand-weavers began to fear for their jobs. In 1768 a mob of them broke into his house, gutted it and destroyed all his machines.

To avoid further trouble, Hargreaves moved to Nottingham where he set up a small cotton mill with a partner, spinning yarn for stocking manufacturers. They made quite a decent living. In the late eighteenth century the world was in desperate need of a spinning machine, so that production of thread could keep up with demand for it from the growing cotton industry. Six years after Hargreaves' death, there were more than 20,000 hand jennies in operation in England.

Hutton, James
"Founder of Geology"

He aged the world

1726-97

In James Hutton's day, most people in Europe believed that the Earth was about six thousand years old, calculated from the book of Genesis in the Bible. It took a lot of nerve for a respectable Scottish businessman and scientist to suggest otherwise.

In a series of papers to the Royal Society of Edinburgh in 1785 he put forward his revolutionary idea - that the processes which formed the surface of the Earth in the past, such as volcanoes or floods, are still going on - that the Earth is still changing and always has done. This is what his theory of *Uniformitarianism* means. As he put it: 'there is no sign of a beginning and no prospect of an end'. He thought of the Earth as a giant heat engine. Heat from the Earth powered the formation of new rocks from volcanoes. Thus, new rocks were being created all the time, just as old rocks were being eroded away by the weather. Basically he was right, but fundamentalist Christians were appalled to think that anyone could suggest that the Earth was so incredibly old.

As well as suggesting Uniformitarianism, Hutton was the first person to realise that warm air holds more moisture than cold air, so that rain falls when a mass of warm air is cooled, usually after meeting a mass of cooler air. His notes also speak of a theory of evolution by natural selection, sixty years before **Darwin** went public.

Cavendish, Henry

Weird scientist who was frightened of women

1731-1810

Henry Cavendish was very brilliant - and very shy. At meetings of the Royal Society* he's described as scurrying from room to room uttering strange shrill cries, looking cross if anyone looked at him, and approaching groups of fellow members to listen to their conversation only to scurry away if anyone spoke to him directly. If he had to talk, he never talked to more than one man at a time - never to women. He used to leave his order for lunch in a written note on the hall table to avoid speaking to the servants and he sacked any maid who came near him. He lived for science and died alone.

He hardly even cared whether people found out about his discoveries - almost none of his work on electricity was published during his lifetime. (His method for testing the voltage of an electric current was to shock himself.) Working alone, he discovered hydrogen and found that water is made of two gases: 'dephlogisticated air (oxygen)' united with 'inflammable air (hydrogen)' as he put it. Phlogiston was then thought to be the stuff of fire.

Later, he measured the mass of the Earth (extremely massive) and what is known as the gravitational constant. This is a number which is needed to calculate the full relationship between the mass of objects, their distance from each other, and the gravitational pull between them. It's one of the most fundamental numbers in the Universe and had been suggested by Isaac Newton, but was then still unknown. Cavendish measured the gravitational constant by means of a two-metre long rod with small lead balls at each end, balanced from a wire. When two great big lumps of metal were placed near the lead balls, the rod turned ever so slightly under their gravitational pull. Cavendish knew the weights of all the items in the experiment and the distance the rod had turned; he knew everything except the gravitational constant, which he could now calculate. Once he knew *that* he could calculate the mass of the Earth - roughly 6,700 million, million, million tons. The Cavendish laboratory in Cambridge was paid for by his descendants.

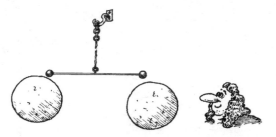

Arkwright, Richard

Inventor of a revolutionary spinning-frame

1732-92

Wool is lovely and warm, but it can be too warm in summer, and it's itchy if worn next to the skin. Cotton is smoother. In the eighteenth century demand for cotton grew fast. But whereas woollen yarn was made in England, cotton yarn came from India. Richard Arkwright designed a machine which could produce cotton yarn in large quantities in England.

Arkwright started his working life as a wigmaker and barber in Lancashire. Being a natural inventor, he soon developed a new process for dying hair. By 1761 he was travelling to 'mop fairs', where servant girls went looking for work, so as to buy their hair. Unfortunately, the strange fashion for wearing wigs was starting to fade. This may have been partly why he turned his attention to cotton.

Cotton thread was still mainly hand-spun in the 1760s. Arkwright saw the possibilities of a machine to replace hand-spinning. He developed his machine in secret, risking all he had in the process, and his clothes were in rags through lack of money by the time he finished. But by 1769 his spinning-frame was ready to be patented*. It produced cotton yarn strong enough for the warp (the long threads) as well as the weft (the cross threads) of cloth. Soon his machines could perform most of the processes needed for making textiles and they could be powered by steam engines. Angry hand-workers rioted, fearful of losing their jobs, but they couldn't stop 'progress'.

Arkwright is also important for another invention, although this invention can't be seen directly. He developed the first 'factory system' for the manufacture of cloth. He built several cotton mills and ended his life with a fortune worth 2.5 million pounds - a huge sum for those days.

Priestley, Joseph

Father of the fizzy drink and 'discoverer' of oxygen

1733-1804

Joseph was a Unitarian minister in Leeds. His house was right next door to a brewery. Being interested in science, he started to collect the gas which is given off in little bubbles when beer ferments and found out that this gas (carbon dioxide), then known as 'fixed air', will dissolve in water under slight pressure to make a fizzy drink, now called 'soda water'. At that time only two gases were known about: air and hydrogen (discovered by **Cavendish**), so this was an important new discovery.

86

Priestley went on to discover several more gases, of which by far the most important was oxygen, in 1774. (Actually it had been discovered by a Swedish chemist, **Karl Scheele**, slightly earlier, but he didn't publish his finding quickly enough, so Priestley got the credit.)

98

Priestley called the gas 'dephlogisticated' air. A popular theory said that burning took place when phlogiston (burning stuff) was given off by the burning substance. Priestley reasoned that, since things burned well in oxygen, that must mean that oxygen lacked phlogiston and drew it from the burning substance. The next year he met **Antoine Lavoisier** in Paris. It was Lavoisier who realised the true importance of the gas and called it oxygen. Priestley went on believing in phlogiston to the bitter end.

100

Priestley was the first person to call rubber 'rubber' - because it rubs things out. He was a member of the Lunar Society*, based in Birmingham. Priestley supported the Americans in the American War of Independence and the revolutionaries in the French Revolution. In 1791 an anti-revolutionary mob burned down his house in Birmingham. The following Sunday, Priestley preached a sermon on the subject: 'Father forgive them for they know not what they do'. But he escaped from Birmingham soon after. He left for America in 1794, never to return.

Mesmer, Franz Anton

Human magnet
who mesmerised his patients

1734-1815

Franz Mesmer, a doctor from the University of Vienna, was interested in astrology, electricity, magnetism - all that seemed most way-out in his lifetime. He believed that the human body contains a mysterious fluid and that disease happens if the fluid can't flow freely. He claimed that the fluid responds to magnetism and that blockages become unblocked if magnets are passed over the body of someone suffering from disease. In accordance with this completely unscientific theory, he began to treat his patients with magnets - and some of them got better. Later, Mesmer stopped using magnets and used just his hands. Some of his patients still got better! He said he was curing them with 'animal magnetism'.

In 1778, after being accused of fraud, he left Vienna for Paris. There he became even more fashionable and successful. French doctors were appalled and the government appointed a commission to look into his claims. Members of the commission included **Antoine Lavoisier**, **Benjamin Franklin** and Joseph Guillotin, who invented the guillotine. Their report was unfavourable and Mesmer had to leave Paris.

Although Mesmer was a bit of a fraud, it seems clear that he managed to cure some of his patients by suggestion, that is, by hypnotising them. We still use the word 'mesmerise' to describe the act of putting someone into a hypnotic trance.

Lagrange, Joseph Louis

French-Italian founder of the metric system

1736-1813

While Joseph Lagrange was a schoolboy he came across an essay on the calculus by the astronomer **Halley** and was fired by an interest in mathematics. He made many important discoveries, working in Turin, then in Berlin and finally, from 1787, at the French Royal Academy in Paris. There he was given an apartment in the Palace of the Louvre and made a fuss of by Marie Antoinette, the wife of Louis XVI.

Two years later, the bloody French Revolution broke out. Both Louis and Marie Antoinette went to the guillotine as did hundreds of lesser nobles. Lagrange, a quiet kindly man, survived unharmed. In 1793, the Revolutionary government put him at the head of a commission to reform the chaotic system of weights and measures then in use in France, where different areas had their own measures. Also on the commission were 100 **Lavoisier** and Laplace.

They came up with the metric system, based on the number ten, the most rational system of measurement ever invented. It centred around the *metre* (Greek *metron*, meaning 'measure'). A *metre* was 1/10,000,000 of a quarter of the circumference of the Earth, passing through the poles and through Paris. A *centimetre* is 1/100 of a metre and a *gram* is the weight of a cubic centimetre of water - and so on. This system became official in France in 1795 and is now accepted in most countries. For a while the French went even further. They had ten-hour days and ten-day weeks, but they gave this up in 1806. Before his death Lagrange was made a count by the Emperor Napoleon.

Watt, James

Inventor of a very efficient steam engine

1736-1819

In 1764 James Watt, a mathematical instrument maker from Glasgow, was asked to repair a model of a **Newcomen** steam engine. Steam engines work by producing a vacuum when steam condenses to water. In the Newcomen engine, a single chamber had to be repeatedly cooled to condense the steam then heated again for the next lot of steam. Watt's brilliant idea was for an engine with two chambers, one always hot for steam and the other always cool for condensing it. This was far more efficient. He went into partnership with the Birmingham industrialist Matthew Boulton and in 1774 he moved to Birmingham. Further improvements followed. He, or his assistants, designed a 'sun-and-planet' gear to convert the up and down movement of the piston to a circular movement. This meant that the Watts engine could now drive most kinds of factory machines. By 1800 there were at least 500 of Boulton and Watts engines in British factories. They powered the industrial revolution and so changed the world.

Watt became a member of the Lunar Society*, based in Birmingham, and was elected a member of the Royal Society*. In his honour the unit of power is named after him. For instance, light bulbs are mostly either 100 watt, 60 watt or 40 watt.

Herschel, Frederick William

Discovered the planet Uranus

1738-1822

William Herschel discovered the planet Uranus in 1781, the first new planet to be discovered since ancient times. He did it with a telescope which he made himself.

He started life as a musician, playing in a regimental band in Hanover, Germany, but in 1757 he moved to England and it was there that he became interested in mathematics and the stars. Unable to afford a big telescope he set out to make his own, grinding his own reflecting mirrors. He was so keen to make the best possible telescope that he threw away 200 mirrors before he was satisfied and once spent sixteen hours without a break polishing one particular mirror to perfection. He cast the larger metal discs in a foundry in the basement of his house. He was helped by his very clever sister **Caroline Herschel**, who discovered eight comets in her own right. She used to spoon morsels of food into William's mouth when he wouldn't stop working.

Herschel made many other discoveries apart from Uranus. He had ideas about galaxies and the universe which were way ahead of his time. With his powerful telescopes he was able to see that some nebulae, milky patches in the sky, were in fact what he called 'island universes' of individual stars - what we now call galaxies. He died at the age of eighty-four years - which happens to be the length of time taken by Uranus to circle the Sun.

Montgolfier, Joseph-Michel & Jacques-Etienne

Frenchmen who invented the hot-air balloon

Joseph-Michel 1740-1810, Jacques-Etienne 1745-99

An ancestor of the Montgolfiers discovered the secret of paper making while being held prisoner in Damascus during the crusades. The family developed a successful paper making business which is why Joseph and Jacques Montgolfier had enough money to pursue their scientific interests.

Air expands as it gets warmer, so it takes up more space, but is spread more thinly and is therefore lighter. It was in 1782 that the Montgolfiers first put this fact to the test and discovered that a lightweight paper or fabric bag will rise if it's filled with hot air. The next year, on 4 June 1783, they made a remarkable demonstration in the market place of the nearby town of Annonay. They burned wool and straw under a large linen bag. The bag sailed upwards to 1,000 metres. It stayed in the air for ten minutes and had travelled nearly 2.5 kilometres (1.5 miles) before it came down again.

Word of this miracle soon reached the French king in Paris, and the Montgolfiers were invited to show their invention to the royal court. On 19 September 1783 at the Palace of Versailles, before King Louis XVI and Queen Marie Antoinette, a sheep, a cock and a duck floated upwards for eight minutes, until they landed 3.2 kilometres (2 miles) away. They were the first flightless animals to fly without the assistance of eagles, whirlwinds and suchlike. Two months later, on 21 November, two human volunteers replaced the animals. The Marquis d'Arlandes and Pilatre de Rozier drifted high above Paris for twenty-five minutes, landing 9 kilometres (5.5 miles) from their take off point. This was the first proper, manned flight in history.

Scheele, Karl Wilhelm

Swedish-German who discovered oxygen

1742-86

Karl Scheele discovered more chemicals in a short space of time than any other chemist before or since - several acids, including citric acid and tartaric acid and a remarkable number of chemical elements*, among them: manganese, tungsten, chlorine, nitrogen - and oxygen. He also discovered oxygen in 1772, two years *before* **Joseph Priestley**. He called it 'fire air' and wrote about it in his only book, *Chemical Observations and Experiments on Air and Fire*. Unfortunately his book wasn't published until 1777, by which time Priestley had published his own results, so Priestley got all the credit.

89

Scheele worked in Sweden all his life. He came from Pomerania, part of Sweden at the time, but usually part of Germany. He never took a post at a university and turned down offers of a position at the royal courts of England and Prussia. He died at the young age of forty-three, possibly of mercury poisoning.

Leblanc, Nicolas

French chemist who gave us soap
1742-1806

Soap was probably invented by the ancient Celts, large fair-haired people who lived in the area around modern Switzerland during the early iron age. They made it from lard and the ashes of plants and called it *saipo* - where the word soap comes from. Until the time of Leblanc, soda ash, the basic ingredient of soap, was still being extracted from wood or seaweed by a slow, primitive process. Lack of soda ash held up industrial development because, apart from soap, soda ash was also used in the manufacture of glass, porcelain and paper. In 1775 the French Academy of Sciences offered a prize to whoever could come up with a process for making soda ash cheaply from salt. Both products are simple compounds of sodium, so it should be possible.

Leblanc won the prize in 1783. For the first time soda ash was cheap and widely available - as was soap. Unfortunately, Leblanc was never paid his prize money. In 1789 the French Revolution started. The revolutionary government, desperate for soda ash, forced Leblanc to make his process public without payment. He sank into poverty and although he was given his factory back in 1800, he was too poor to get it up and running. He killed himself in 1806.

Lavoisier, Antoine Laurent
"Father of modern chemistry"

French chemist who discovered what burning is

1743-94

89 98 Antoine Lavoisier didn't discover oxygen, **Joseph Priestley** and, separately, **Karl Scheele** did that. But when Priestley met Lavoisier in Paris in 1775 and told him of his discovery, it was Lavoisier who immediately understood how important it was. At that time it was thought that everything that burned contained phlogiston - burning stuff. Burning happened when phlogiston was released into the air. The ash or residue had no phlogiston left in it and so could burn no more. Lavoisier completely demolished the phlogiston theory and so cleared the way for modern chemistry to develop. He called the newly-discovered gas 'oxygen' and showed that combustion (burning) is what happens when oxygen combines with whatever is being burnt. He showed that air is a mixture of gases, one of which is oxygen, and that respiration (breathing of oxygen by plants and animals) is similar to combustion.

Lavoisier is thought of as the father of modern chemistry. All his experiments were carefully measured - he once even burned a diamond in order to weigh the ash (1772). He worked out the 'law of conservation of mass', a basic idea in chemistry - that in a chemical reaction there's always as much stuff in total at the end as at the beginning, even if it's in a different form. As if these discoveries weren't enough, he helped develop a system of chemical names. His system is so clear and logical that it's still in use today. The names show what something is made of: for instance, 'carbon dioxide' is made of one atom of carbon and two of oxygen (the 'di' means 'two').

After the French Revolution broke out in 1789, Lavoisier was elected on to the Paris commune, which then governed Paris. He arranged for a wall to be built around the town to keep out smuggled goods. In 1793, the ferocious revolutionary leader Jean-Paul Marat accused him of 'stopping the circulation of air' and of 'imprisoning' the town with the wall. Those were crazy days. Marat was assassinated in his bath later that year, but the damage was done. Lavoisier went to the guillotine on 8 May 1794 after a trial which lasted less than a day. As the arresting officer put it: 'The Republic has no need of scientists'.

Banks, Joseph

Plant specialist who visited Australia

1743-1820

Joseph Banks was a botanist, a specialist in plants. In 1766 he travelled to Newfoundland where he collected many undiscovered specimens. On his return he was elected a member of the Royal Society*. Two years later he was off again, this time with Captain Cook on his famous voyage around the world (1768-71). Banks was a wealthy man, having inherited money from his father, so he was able to pay for an assistant, four artists and all the equipment he needed to share the voyage with him. 'Botany Bay' near modern Sydney got its name due to his excitement at finding so many new plants when they landed there in 1770. He returned to England with 3,600 plants, 1,400 of them never before classified.

From 1778 until his death he was president of the Royal Society*. He sent many other botanists on collecting expeditions to far off corners of the world.

Cartwright, Reverend Edmund

Vicar with vision of a loom
1743-1823

By 1787 the Industrial Revolution was taking off. **Hargreaves** invented his spinning jenny in 1764, **Richard Arkwright** invented his spinning frame in 1769 and **Samuel Crompton** invented his 'mule' in 1779. What was lacking was an industrial weaving machine.

84
88
111

The Reverend Edmund Cartwright built his power loom without ever having seen an ordinary hand loom. He patented* it in 1785. It could be powered by water and later by steam, and promised to be far more efficient than hand-looms which were still in general use. Then in 1789 he invented a wool-combing machine which could do the work of twenty hand-combers. Hand-workers were already afraid of losing their jobs and this was the last straw. Crowds of workers demonstrated against the wool-combing machine, and that same year a Manchester factory which had bought four hundred of his power looms was burned down.

Cartwright never stopped inventing. Among other things he invented a steam engine and a reaping machine. He helped his friend **Robert Fulton** to develop a steamship. But he never made much money from his inventions. In fact he went bankrupt in 1793 and had to sell his factory. Luckily, in 1809 Parliament voted for him to be given £10,000.

117

Lamarck, Jean-Baptiste, Chevalier de

He evolved a theory
1744-1829

Question: why do giraffes have long necks?
Answer: so that they can eat the leaves off trees.

Ah - but how do they get them? There are no plastic surgeons to offer neck-lengthening operations to giraffes, even if giraffes had the money. Jean Baptiste Lamarck's answer to this problem was the very first sensible theory of evolution. It wasn't the right theory, but at least it was a theory.

In 1781, Jean Baptiste, Chevalier de (Knight of) Lamarck, the thirteenth son of a poor French nobleman, was made official botanist to King Louis XIV. In 1793 he became a professor at the Museum of Natural History in Paris, in the invertebrate department. The great Swedish naturalist, **Linnaeus**, had categorised most animals but he'd left the invertebrates (animals without backbones) in a mess. There were even some scientists who grouped crocodiles with insects! Lamarck categorised invertebrates separately from vertebrates. He also coined the word 'biology'.

As a result of his studies Lamarck realised that the world is incredibly old. And he came to believe that living things have evolved into different species* in small steps over a similar huge period. Where he was wrong was in thinking that this evolution of species is caused by the 'inheritance of acquired characteristics' - that

81

animals pass on to their young the changes which have happened to them due to exercise during their lives. According to his theory, organs which are used a lot get bigger and stronger over the generations, and those that are only used a little wither and fade away. Thus his answer to the giraffe problem: he thought that giraffes have grown long necks because generations of them have stretched up into trees to browse. This theory is called 'Lamarckism'. Unfortunately it fails to explain many things: how a leopard gets its spots, for instance - you can hardly *try* to get spots.

Despite all his work for science, Lamarck ended his life as unsuccessfully as his most famous theory. He died poor and blind.

Volta, Alessandro Giuseppe, Count

Italian who invented the battery

1745-1827

Alessandro Volta became interested in electricity after reading a book on the subject by **Joseph Priestley**. In

1775 he invented a device for generating static electricity, called the *electrophorus*.

The problem with static is that there's no steady electric current, so it's not as useful as it ought to be. In 1780, Volta's friend, Luigi Galvani, discovered that a dead frog's leg lying between two pieces of metal twitched and produced an electric current. Galvani, being a biologist, thought that the current was produced by the frog.

Volta proved otherwise. He became convinced that the current was produced by the two different metals and the salty liquids of the frog. In 1800 he made a pile of zinc and silver discs separated by cloth or paper which had been soaked in brine (salty water), and found that it produced an electric current. This voltaic 'pile' was the first ever battery ('battery' because a battery is any group of things acting together, such as a battery of guns). As a variation on the 'pile' he also connected glasses of brine by hoops of metal, made of copper at one end and zinc at the other. He demonstrated these connected 'cells' before the Emperor Napoleon in 1801, thus starting the age of electricity.

Napoleon showered honours on Volta, who came from a noble but poor Italian family, but the greatest honour he received is that the unit of force which drives an electric current is named after him - the volt.

Jenner, Edward

Doctor who conquered smallpox

1749-1823

Smallpox is deadly. Large numbers of people used to die of it every year. Almost worse, those that survived were often 'pockmarked', their faces hideously ravaged with scars. Many feared this more than death.

For hundreds of years, the Turks and the Chinese had known that a mild dose of smallpox would often protect the sufferer from a more deadly attack. Pus from the blisters of someone suffering a mild attack was given to a healthy person. Unfortunately, the healthy person might not necessarily suffer a mild dose of the disease. The cure was almost more dangerous than the disease itself. It was a gamble. Nevertheless, this practice spread to Europe where it was known as inoculation.

Jenner, an English country doctor, knew of a popular tradition that people who had had cowpox (which is far less dangerous) didn't catch smallpox. In 1796 he infected an eight-year-old boy called James Phipps with cowpox taken from a girl who had this milder illness. James duly caught the cowpox.

Two months later Jenner infected him with deadly smallpox, which James didn't catch (fortunately!).

Jenner called his new technique 'vaccination' after *vaccinia*, the Latin for cowpox. Smallpox was the first major disease to be conquered by medicine. By 1805 the number of deaths from smallpox in Britain was down by two thirds. In the rest of the world there was similar success.

Appert, Nicolas-Francois

Father of canned food

around 1750-1841

In 1795 the armies of revolutionary France under Napoleon swept across Europe, winning a series of massive victories. They travelled so far and so fast that it was a problem to keep them (and the French navy) fed. The French government offered a prize of 12,000 francs to whoever could solve the problem.

For the next fourteen years Nicolas Appert, a French chef and sweet-maker, tried out hundreds of different ways of preserving food. By trial and error he realised that heating food to boiling point and then sealing it in airtight containers would stop it going rotten. (This was

years before **Louis Pasteur,** so no one knew *why* food went rotten.) In 1804 Appert opened the world's first cannery to produce food in sealed glass containers. His discovery was a huge advance.

He published his findings in 1810 and won the 12,000 francs. Unfortunately he lost everything after Napoleon's final defeat in 1815 (although the factory that he founded kept going until 1933). In the year that he won his prize, Peter Durand, an Englishman, patented* the world's first tin-coated cast-iron can, which together with Appert's methods of heating, led to the modern canned food industry.

Herschel, Caroline Lucretia

First famous woman astronomer

1750-1848

Caroline Herschel was a musician as well as an astronomer. Born in Hanover, Germany, she was taught the violin secretly by her father against the wishes of her mother. When her father died, she escaped the domestic life her mother had planned for her by going to live with her brother William in Bath, England.

William Herschel was then a music teacher but would soon become a famous astronomer. In England Caroline is said to have learned to sing by copying violin music with a gag between her teeth. It seems to have worked - she became a successful singer.

Meanwhile William was becoming obsessed by the stars. Caroline helped him, often staying up all night. She did most of his calculations. Soon she too was obsessed. She trawled the heavens with her own telescope, and became a famous astronomer in her own right, in fact the first major woman astronomer. By the time she died, back in Germany at the grand old age of ninety-seven, she had catalogued 2,500 nebulae, a great many star clusters and had discovered eight comets.

Jacquard, Joseph-Marie

Inventor of a loom
1752-1834

Weavers can cope all right with simple patterns. But how can a weaver's simple loom weave something complicated, like a pattern of flowers for instance? Until Jacquard came along, the answer was - it can't. Such complicated designs had to be either hand-woven or embroidered, which takes forever.

Joseph Jacquard was a silk weaver from Lyon in France. Silk was a luxury fabric and ideal for complicated, luxurious designs. With the help of a Jacquard loom, a single weaver could weave complicated designs relatively quickly. The design was marked out as a pattern of holes punched into a series of stiff pieces of card. The holes in the cards controlled which threads the machine would weave with each pass of the loom.

Jacquard first thought of his idea in 1790 during the bloody height of the French Revolution. In 1801 the

Emperor Napoleon invited him to Paris to demonstrate it. With Napoleon's support the design spread like wildfire, even though silk workers, frightened for their jobs, burned the looms and attacked Jacquard. By 1812 there were 11,000 Jacquard looms in operation in France, and the weaving of luxury fabrics is still a major industry there.

Crompton, Samuel

Inventor who could spin a yarn

1753-1827

Samuel Crompton's family lived in rooms in an old mansion called the Hall-in-the-Wood near Bolton in Lancashire. After his father died, when Samuel was only five, the rest of the family had to work hard to make ends meet. Every day after school, Samuel spun or wove. Spinning was annoying work because the thread on his hand-operated spinning-jenny kept breaking.

Working at night, and supporting himself by spinning and playing the fiddle at Bolton Theatre, Crompton developed a new spinning machine. It was a mixture of **Arkwright's** frame
88
84 and **Hargreaves'** spinning-jenny, together with an invention of his own, which copied the movements of a hand-spinner's left hand. His machine was called the Hall-in-the-Wood wheel at first, but soon became known as 'Crompton's Mule', because like a mule it was a cross-breed of two earlier inventions. It could spin yarn which was finer than expensive Indian imports and it gave a huge boost to Britain's textile industry.

Crompton couldn't afford a patent*. He gave his machine to a group of local manufacturers in return for a promise of payment - and got just £67. By 1812 there were at least 4,600,000 spindles turning on Crompton's Mules in Britain, but Crompton was poor as a church mouse. Parliament gave him £5,000 in thanks for his services to the country. Unfortunately, he didn't do well in business and may have taken to drink towards the end of his life.

Murdock, William

Father of gas lights
1754-1839

In 1792 William Murdock, a Scottish engineer, heated coal in the absence of air, a process similar to making charcoal from wood. The coal gave off gases which Murdock collected and he discovered that these gases burn very easily. He was quick to see the possibilities. Unlike solid coal, coal *gas* could flow along pipes, which had to be useful. He tried out various designs of gas lamp and developed ways of storing the gas in gasometers.

For most of his life, Murdock worked for the firm of Boulton and **Watt**, developing the steam engine and various other inventions. By 1803 he had lit their factory in Soho Birmingham with gas light and by 1807 some of London's streets had gas lighting. Other towns soon followed and by the end of the century almost every large town in Britain had its own gas works, producing coal gas for street lighting.

Murdock became a member of the Lunar Society* along with Boulton and Watt.

94

McAdam, John Loudon

Scotsman who built roads

1756-1836

Travel in the eighteenth century was dangerous, dirty and, above all, slow. British roads had been in a terrible condition since the time of the Romans.

John McAdam was a Scots engineer who made money in New York during the American War of Independence as agent in charge of selling captured American ships. After the revolutionaries won, he returned to Britain with his fortune and bought an estate in Ayrshire. He became 'road trustee' for his local district. He'd always had an interest in roads, in fact he built a model road as a schoolboy in Scotland, and now he could afford to experiment with road surfaces around his small estate. He came to the conclusion that roads should be slightly raised above the surrounding land, with drains on either side and built with a slight curve, or camber, so that rainwater can drain off. The base of the road should be of largish, hard stone and the surface should be of small stones, as square as possble, all about the same size and none weighing more than 170 grams.

In 1815 McAdam became surveyor general of the roads of Bristol. He was so successful that in 1827 he was made surveyor general for all the roads of Britain.

Between 1798 and 1814 McAdam travelled 48,000 kilometres (30,000 miles) of British roads in the course of his duties, a total of two thousand days (5.5 years) on the road. He usually travelled in a closed two-horse carriage, followed by his Newfoundland dog and a pony which he used for off-road excursions. His 'macadamised' roads transformed travel on most British main roads. His fame spread and all over Europe countries followed the British example - and still do, although now the macadam is mixed with tar or asphalt to make 'tarmac'.

Telford, Thomas

British bridge builder

1757-1834

Thomas Telford was a Scottish engineer, the son of a poor shepherd. He was born in a cottage and trained as a mason. Later he became an architect and an engineer. He laid more than 1,450 kilometres (900 miles) of Scottish roads, built 1,200 Scottish bridges, and built the main road from Chester to Holyhead (now the A5). He also designed the Caledonian canal, built several large aqueducts to carry canals over valleys, designed the St. Katharine's Docks in London, and most famously, built the Menai Suspension Bridge joining the Isle of

Anglesey to the mainland of Wales. The road dangles beneath sixteen massive 23.75 ton chains and was the wonder of its time.

Niepce, Joseph Nicéphore

Inventor of photography
1765-1833

Niepce fought in Napoleon's armies, then became adminstrator of Nice, where he settled down to full time invention. He invented an early internal-combustion engine powered by lycopodium powder, made from fungus spores and used in fireworks.

In 1813 he began work on his greatest project. It grew from an interest in lithography, which was a new printing technique in the early 1800s. In lithography the image to be printed is drawn in grease on to a stone. When the stone is dampened, ink sticks to the grease but not to the wet stone. Unfortunately, Niepce couldn't draw for toffee. He looked for ways to capture an image directly on the stone, using sunlight. By 1822 he'd produced a picture from an engraving, using a bitumen-coated pewter plate. Bitumen hardens in sunlight and pewter is a metal which can be engraved for printing. He called his process 'heliography', (sun-drawing, from *helios*, the Greek for sun). He then had the further idea of projecting light through a pinhole camera on to the plate. Finally, in 1826/7, he took a picture from his attic window. The exposure took eight hours, but this was the first ever photograph. The plate still exists and is kept at the University of Texas.

Niepce's invention was never practical as it stood. In 1829 he went into partnership with the artist, **Louis Jacques Daguerre**, but he didn't live long enough to see the results of their combined efforts.

133

Fulton, Robert

American who sailed a steamship
1765-1815

Robert Fulton built the world's first successful steamship. It was launched on the Hudson River in 1807 and was called - *Steamboat*. *Steamboat* steamed from New York to Albany in just 32 hours at the impressive speed of 7.6 kph (4.7 mph). Sailing ships took four days for the same journey, so this was a big improvement. The next year, *Steamboat* was widened, stiffened and renamed the *Clermont*. The age of steamships had arrived.

Fulton also built submarines. In 1800 the Napoleonic Wars between Britain and France were raging. He offered to build a submarine for the French. At first they refused because they thought sneaking around under water wasn't a good way to fight. He built one, the *Nautilus*, anyway. The French then gave him permission to attack two British ships. Unfortunately, or fortunately depending which side you're on, the British ships sailed away before he could get near them.

Nothing daunted, in 1804 Fulton offered to build a submarine - for the British. It made two unsuccessful attacks on French ships. However, by that time, it was obvious to everyone that Britain was winning the war and they had no need for Fulton's submarines. That's when he went back to the USA and started building *Steamboat*. Later, in 1815, he built a steam warship, *USS Fulton* also called *USS Demologos*. It never saw action and was accidentally blown up in 1829.

Whitney, Eli

Inventor of a cotton gin

1765-1825

In the late 1700s English cotton mills were hungry for cotton. Their main source of supply was the southern United States. Along the coast the Americans grew black seed cotton. It was easy to separate the lint (fibre) from the seed of black seed cotton. Inland, they grew green seed cotton. The lint of green seed cotton stuck to the seed and it was a long, hard process to separate the two. Eli Whitney saw that a machine which could separate green seed cotton could make him a fortune.

Whitney's cotton gin was simple and effective. Hundreds of short wire hooks were set on a roller in just the right positions to poke through the holes in a flat wire mesh. Raw cotton was poured from a hopper on to the mesh. The holes were small enough to stop cotton seed being pulled through, but big enough to let the lint get hooked and be pulled through to the other side. A revolving brush then removed the lint from the hooks so that they could hook up more.

Whitney never got rich from his invention. It was too easy to copy. Instead, he made another invention, harder to see but even more important. In 1797 he turned his hand to gun making. He bid to supply the United States government with 10,000 muskets in two years. Up until that time muskets had been individually crafted. You couldn't take the trigger from one and fit it to another, even if they were of the same design. Whitney designed machine tools which could be operated by quite unskilled men and which could produce identical parts. He could thus divide the labour of production into small and separate tasks, and all the bits could be fitted together at the end. He had invented mass production.

Macintosh, Charles

Inventor of the mackintosh

1766-1843

The mackintosh was invented by a Scotsman. Hardly surprising, as Scotland is one of the rainiest countries in the world. In 1823, Charles Macintosh, a Scottish chemist, was looking into ways of using the waste products of the gas industry - gas was made from coal in those days. He tried distilling (boiling off) tar from the coal residues. A by-product of distillation was a chemical called 'coal naptha'. Now coal naptha dissolves india-rubber. Macintosh dissolved rubber in coal naptha and used the mixture to stick two pieces of cloth together. The result was a strong, waterproof material.

Garments made of mackintosh sold like hot cakes, even though early mackintoshes tended to leak at the seams - and went stiff in winter and sticky in summer. (This problem was solved once vulcanised rubber, invented by **Charles Goodyear**, became available in 1839.) Travellers on stage coaches now had some decent protection from the rain if they were travelling on the stage coach roof. Sales only tailed off with the coming of trains which provided plenty of space for people to sit inside.

140

Dalton, John

Englishman who believed in atoms
1766-1844

You can think of Dalton's universe as a jumble of billions and billions of tiny marbles. Each marble of the same element* has the same weight as other marbles of that element. Dalton called them 'atoms', the word used by the Ancient Greek thinker **Democritus**. Other modern scientists, such as **Boyle**, had suggested that gases might be made of particles, but Dalton was the first modern scientist to suggest that *everything* is made up of tiny particles.

13
62

This is how it happened. Dalton kept notes on the weather for fifty-seven years (200,000 entries by the time he died). Being interested in the weather he was naturally interested in air, since that's mainly what the weather is made up of. And because air is a mixture of gases he became interested in gases.

The next step was to realise that when two gases combine to make a new gas, they always do so in exactly the same proportions, for instance one gramme of one particular gas to two grams of another gas. Dalton saw that this might be because their atoms weigh differently in the same proportions. In the above case, one atom of the second gas would be twice as heavy as an atom of the first. Suddenly it was clear as daylight - his theory could be used to explain how *all* elements, and not just gases, combine to form chemical compounds. He drew up the first table of atomic weights of elements.

Dalton was the son of a Quaker weaver. He never went to University - Quakers and other dissenters* weren't allowed to, and he was colour blind. Due to his studies of colour blindness, Daltonism is another word for the condition.

Cuvier, Georges Léopold, Baron

He boned up on bones
1769-1832

Palaeontology is the study of dusty old bones dug from dusty old rocks. Sounds boring, but isn't. For starters, without palaeontology we wouldn't know about the dinosaurs. Georges Cuvier, a French scientist who worked at the Museum of Natural History in Paris, was the first person to study old bones scientifically. He became incredibly skilled at fitting old bones together and only just failed to identify the dinosaurs.

148 This was all long before **Charles Darwin** published his theory of evolution by natural selection. From his studies of bones, Cuvier realised that many thousands of species* of animals have died out (become extinct) over the ages. But somehow he had to square this with

his religious belief that the Bible gives a true history of the creation of life. He suggested that species* die out due to major disasters and that after each disaster a whole new bunch of creatures is created by God. According to him, the last such disaster had been the flood described in the Bible, when Noah built his ark.

81 Cuvier developed **Linnaeus'** system of grouping or 'classifying' animals. His system recognised that living things don't form a ladder or chain rising from the lowest, slitheriest worm at one end to human beings at the other; they form a tree with lots of branches, one twig of which is the human species. In his system the animals were divided into four great groups or *phyla* with an extra *phylum* (singular of *phyla*) for creatures which didn't fit in. He broke new ground by classifying the living and the extinct species together. That system (with changes) is still used today. Nowadays there are at least twenty-four different *phyla*.

Trevithick, Richard

Inventor of the first railway engine

1771-1833

Richard Trevithick was an engineer, a champion wrestler and an inventor. His father was the manager of a Cornish coal mine, and it was this which led to his most important invention. He grew up fascinated by the
75 **Newcomen** engine used to pump out his father's mine.

The leap from stationary steam pump to a moving steam engine had been taken as early as 1770 by a French inventor. But the Frenchman's steam road carriage took quarter of an hour to travel a mile and was voted a public nuisance. Trevithick's invention was vastly better. It worked on high-pressure steam, unlike the **Watt** engines then coming into use in mines and factories. The first working model was ready in 1797. Trevethick showed it to his friends on the kitchen table. Four years later he built a full-size road carriage, *Puffing Devil*. After several problems, including leaving it burn out while he and his friends were in the pub, he drove it successfully, reaching a top speed of 17 kph (12 mph).

In 1804 Trevithick rode one of his steam engines on metal rails in a mine in Wales. Four years later he took his new invention to London. *Catch-me-who-can* ran on circular rails at what is now Euston Square. The public paid to ride in its small carriage. Unfortunately, after a while, one of the rails broke and the train fell over. Trevithick was a hopeless businessman.

He went on to design steam-powered paddle boats, threshing machines and a dredger. In 1816 he sailed to Peru and made money bringing steam pumps to the Peruvian silver mines, but he lost it all again during the Peruvian war of independence from Spain. He nearly drowned in a river, was rescued with a lassoo, and was finally given money to get back to England by the son of **Stephenson** who happened to be in South America at the time. He died poor. Local workmen stumped up the money so that the great inventor wouldn't be buried in a pauper's grave.

Senefelder, Alois

Discoverer of lithography
1771-1834

Most printing nowadays, this book for instance, is done by lithography, from the Greek *lithos* meaning a stone. The process was discovered in 1796 by a German actor called Senefelder, then working in Prague, who wanted to publish his own plays.

Senefelder tried to engrave his own copper printing plates, but wasn't very good at it. Then one day in 1796 he happened to jot down his laundry list with a grease pencil on a piece of limestone (as one does!). It occurred to him that stone might offer a way around the problem of engraving. Limestone is easily eaten away by acid. Using acid, he could burn or 'etch' away the surface of the stone where it was unprotected by the lines from the grease pencil. He would end up with a raised surface where the lines had been drawn. Ink could be rolled on the raised surface and he could print the image.

As it turned out, this was barking up the wrong tree. Senefelder worked on his invention for two years and finally arrived at the lithographic process used today, which is actually much easier. All that was necessary was to mark the image in grease on a flat stone, wet the stone and then roll ink on to it. The ink stuck to the grease, but not to the wet stone, and paper pressed against it took up the ink from the grease marks.

Brown, Robert

Naturalist who named the nucleus

1773-1858

Robert Brown was a Scottish naturalist. He travelled to Australia in 1801 and later wrote a huge work on Australian plants. He's famous for two things:

1. He discovered that certain plant cells* have a small lump inside them. He called this lump the *nucleus*, which is Latin for 'little nut'. Nowadays we know that most living cells have a nucleus.

2. In 1831 he was looking at pollen grains mixed in water through a microscope and realised that they were moving about. He looked at other tiny particles in water, both living pollen and other specks of non-living stuff. All moved. This natural, non-stop, random movement of tiny, solid particles in liquids or gases is now called Brownian motion. Brown himself had no idea what caused it. Today we know that it's caused by molecules of the liquid or gas bashing into the solid particles. It's important evidence for the theory that things are made of atoms.

Ampère, André Marie

French scientist whom 'amps' are named after

1775-1836

André Ampère's life was miserable. His father was guillotined during the French Revolution, his first wife died young and his second marriage was a disaster. The words (in Latin) 'happy at last' were written on his gravestone. Which is all a shame because he was brilliant. He's now thought of as the founder of the science of electromagnetism (in his day called electrodynamics - the science of electric currents in motion).

128 In 1820 the experiments of **Hans Oersted**, a Danish scientist, were first published. Oersted showed that if a wire carrying an electric current is held near a compass needle, the needle changes direction - thus proving that magnetism and electricity are related to each other. Within days of reading Oersted's results, Ampère had worked out some of the fundamental principles of how magnetism and electricity affect each other, including his famous right-hand screw rule.

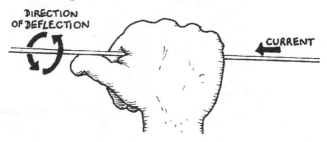

DIRECTION OF DEFLECTION

CURRENT

He also showed that if two wires are lined up parallel to each other, but with electric current flowing in opposite directions, they will repel each other. If their currents flow the same way, they will attract each other. From this it was a small step to imagining how wire wound up in the shape of a spring would behave like a magnet. He called this theoretical object a *solenoid* - an electromagnet.

Ampère was also the first person to find a way to measure electrical current - using a magnetic needle. Today the 'amp' or 'ampère' is the standard unit for measuring the size of an electric current - and a better way to remember him than by what he had on his gravestone.

Oersted, Hans Christian

He introduced a magnet to electricity
1777-1851

Hans Oersted was a professor at the University of Copenhagen and the elder brother of a future (and very unpopular) prime minister of Sweden. He believed that it should be possible to convert all physical forces, such as movement, heat, gravity, magnetism and electricity, from one to another. As early as 1813 he predicted that an electric current should produce a magnetic field, but it wasn't until 1820 that he proved his theory. During one of his lectures, he held a compass needle near to a wire which was connected to a battery. The compass needle swung round so that it pointed at right angles to the current. When he reversed the current the needle pointed the other way. There could be no doubt that the needle was responding to the electric current.

In actual fact, the experiment had been tried in 1802 by an Italian, Gian Romagnosi, but Romagnosi's results were published in a little-known journal, so Oersted got the credit. For a time, the unit of strength of a magnetic field was named after him.

Davy, Humphry

Gas guzzler who invented a lamp
1778-1829

Humphry Davy was said to be the most handsome of all great scientists. He's famous for inventing the Davy lamp, a safety lamp for miners and for discovering several chemical elements*.

His interest in science started early. He lost his first job, at an apothecary's (chemist's) in Cornwall, by causing explosions when he should have been working. Later, while working for a doctor who was interested in the medical properties of gases, he discovered the effects of laughing gas (nitrous oxide). It feels a bit like being drunk, and nitrous oxide parties became quite fashionable for a while.

Seven years later (1807-8), now a lecturer at the Royal Institution in London, he became interested in how electricity causes chemical reactions. By passing electric currents through molten metals and liquid solutions, he discovered sodium, potassium, calcium, magnesium, strontium and barium.

The Davy lamp, which he invented in 1815, gave off light without risk of setting fire to the dangerous gases which lurk in mines, which had been the problem with the candles used by miners until that time. In Davy's lamp the flame burned within a cylinder of metallic gauze so that the heat of the flame was absorbed by the gauze. He also invented the world's first electric light, the arc lamp. However, in 1813 he'd already made what many people think was his greatest discovery of all - he 136 took on **Michael Faraday** as his assistant. Faraday was an even greater scientist than his discoverer.

Somerville, Mary

Early woman science writer
1780-1872

Even as a young girl in Scotland Mary Somerville was brilliantly clever. She learned Latin so as to be able to 67 read **Isaac Newton's** *Principia*.

She became famous after writing a book about the work of Laplace. Honours were showered on her and she became a member of the Royal Society*. Her last book *Molecular and Microscopic Science* was published when she was in her eighty-ninth year. Somerville College in Oxford, the first college for women at the University, is named after her.

Stephenson, George

Inventor who built the first useful steam train

1781-1848

The world's first passenger train service opened for business on the Stockton to Darlington railway line on 27 September 1825. By 1917, less than a hundred years later, more than a million miles of railway track had been laid around the world. The engine which pulled that first train service was the *Active*, designed by George Stephenson. It pulled 450 passengers in 38 carriages at 24 kph (15 mph). This was the first time in human history that passengers were able to travel faster than a galloping horse. Stephenson's train ran on flanged wheels (common to all modern trains) which were his own invention.

After the *Active*, he became engineer for a new railway planned to run between Liverpool and Manchester. His new locomotive, the *Rocket*, could travel at up to 58 kph (36 mph). People weren't used to these sorts of speeds. At the grand opening on 15 September 1830, the MP William Huskisson was run over and later died. The world's first railway accident had also arrived.

Stephenson came from a humble background. His father worked as fireman on a steam powered pump in the Northumberland coal mines. Young George used to help his father and became fascinated by engines when still a boy. He learned to read, put himself through night school and became an engineer. He wasn't the first

123 person to design a steam train - **Trevithick** was earlier - but his designs were more practical, and it's Stephenson who really started the railway revolution.

Bessel, Friedrich Wilhelm

He expanded the Universe
1784-1846

In 1810 King Frederick William III of Prussia commanded a young scientist called Friedrich Bessel to direct the building of a new astronomical observatory at Königsberg. Bessel was director of the observatory for the rest of his life. His measurements of the stars were the most accurate ever taken to that date. By 1818 he was ready to publish a catalogue of over 50,000 stars.

In 1838 Bessel turned his telescope on a nearby star, 61 Cygni. 61 Cygni seems to rock slowly back and forth in the sky. This apparent rocking movement of heavenly bodies is called parallax. It's due to the fact that the observer on Earth is himself moving back and forth as Earth circles the Sun. By measuring the tiny width of Cygni's rocking against the positions of more distant stars behind it, Bessel could work out that 61 Cygni is approximately 35,000,000,000,000 miles away - roughly 6
67 light years*. This was a revolutionary discovery. **Isaac Newton** had thought that the total width of the entire universe might not be more than 2 light years. Due to Bessel, the Universe was now three times bigger than it had been.

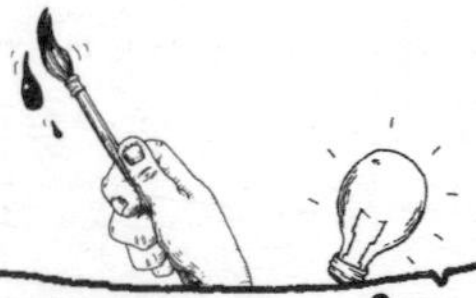

Daguerre, Louis Jacques Mandé

Pioneer of photography

1787-1851

Science is like a dog race and scientists are the greyhounds. In the 1800s there were several greyhounds racing to be first to develop a practical system of photography. First off was the Frenchman,
116 **Joseph Niepce**. He dreamed up the idea of making an image by using light-sensitive material around 1820 and took the world's first ever photograph in 1826. It was a view from his attic bedroom taken after an eight hour exposure. Next came another Frenchman, Louis Daguerre, who developed the first ever practical photographic system (1838), followed by a whisker by
141 the Englishman **Fox Talbot**.

Daguerre was a talented scene painter at the Paris opera. He worked on photography with Niepce from 1829 until Niepce died in 1833. He then continued on his own, and finally developed the 'daguerrotype'. Daguerrotypes were made by exposing a copper plate coated in silver nitrate to light. The plate was then developed in fumes of mercury and 'fixed' by dunking it in a solution of common salt. The resulting image was pale but finely detailed.

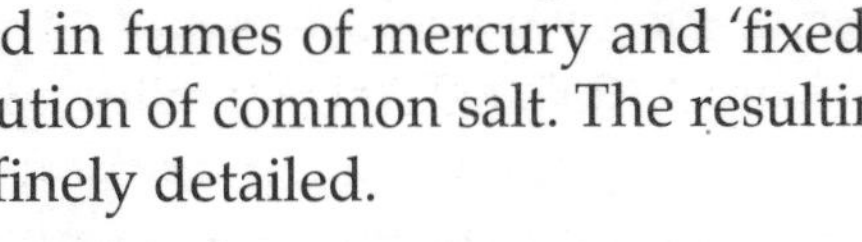

Ohm, Georg Simon

German who resisted currents

1789-1854

The unit of electrical resistance is named after a German scientist called Georg Ohm. Ohm started out as a teacher in a German high school but wanted a post at university level. Unfortunately, he had no formal scientific training and he had to complete some useful research in order to prove himself. He decided to make a detailed investigation of the flow of electric current. He made his own wires and compared the flow of current down wires of different lengths and thicknesses. He discovered that the flow of current depended on how much metal there was for the current to spread out in, and how far the current had to travel. (**Cavendish** had discovered this fifty years before, but then Cavendish often failed to publish the results of his experiments.)

From this work, Ohm arrived at Ohm's Law (1827). This states that the flow of electrical current increases or decreases in direct proportion to the potential difference (voltage), but in inverse proportion to the resistance (now measured in ohms). So half the resistance means twice the flow, and twice the voltage means twice the flow.

Despite this triumph, Ohm was refused a university position. Due to opposition to his ideas, he even had to resign as a teacher. After six years on the breadline his achievement was at last recognised. In 1849 he became a professor at the University of Munich. There's now a street in Munich named after him, as well as the 'ohm'.

Morse, Samuel Finley Breese

Inventor of morse code
1791-1872

Samuel Morse was an artist. He painted some of the best portraits ever painted in America. One day in 1832, in the mid-Atlantic while returning from an art-study trip to Europe, he got into conversation with a fellow passenger, the American inventor, Charles Jackson. Both Jackson and Morse were interested in electricity which was then a little-understood and mysterious force. It occurred to Morse (or Jackson - Jackson claimed that it was his idea) that an electric current together with a magnet could be used to carry messages. By 1835 Morse had built a working model of his invention: electric current flowed down a wire, causing an electromagnet to move a piece of soft iron attached to a pen or pencil. The pen or pencil then wrote on to a moving paper roll.

Morse was a clever man with a gift for friendship. He lobbied hard among friends and politicians for money and political support in order to build an electric telegraph line between Baltimore and Washington, which is over 64 kilometres (40 miles). On 11 May 1844 the first ever telegraph message 'What God hath wrought!' was sent down this wire in a code, Morse code, which Morse invented in 1838. A series of long or short electric pulses was written out at the other end as dots or dashes. Groups of these dots and dashes stood for letters of the alphabet and punctuation marks.

The advantages of Morse's invention were obvious to almost everyone. Within four years of that first message, 8,000 kilometres (5,000 miles) of telegraph lines had been strung up across America. The age of instant communication had begun.

Faraday, Michael

Scientist who invented the electric motor

1791-1867

Michael Faraday was the son of a blacksmith. Although very poor, he was able to teach himself science while working for a bookbinder. His boss allowed him to read the books as well as bind them.

129 In 1813 he became assistant to **Humphry Davy**, a leading scientist at the 'Royal Institution'. Davy's wife treated young Faraday like a servant, but he ignored her rudeness and worked hard in Davy's laboratory. He washed bottles at first, but soon he was helping with research. Davy realised that his young assistant was destined to become an even greater scientist than he was himself - something that Davy could never accept. In 1824 Faraday was elected to the Royal Society* against Davy's opposition. He became one of the greatest British scientists.

Faraday invented ways to liquify gases at very low temperatures, he discovered benzene and made important discoveries in electrolysis - chemical reaction produced by electric current. But above all, he invented the first electric generator and discovered the scientific laws which govern the relationship between electricity and magnetism.

Like many scientists of his time, Faraday was fired by
128 **Oersted's** demonstration of how an electric current will deflect a magnetic needle (1819). Faraday realised that if an electric current could affect a magnet, then a magnet might produce an electric current. He mounted a copper wheel so that its rim passed between the poles of a magnet. Sure enough, when the wheel was turned, a current was produced in the copper, which could be led off down a wire. He'd made the world's first electric generator. The same principle lies behind the massive electricity generators which power our modern electric grids. Although nowadays, the modern equivalent of Faraday's copper wheel is turned mostly by steam turbines powered by gas, coal or oil.

Babbage, Charles

Englishman who engineered an early computer

1791-1871

In 1823 Charles Babbage persuaded the British government to give him the money to start work on a mechanical calculating machine. Babbage was a member of the Royal Society*, but even so it was remarkable that the government could be persuaded to part with money for something so unusual. **Blaise Pascal** had invented a simple calculating machine as early as 1641, but Babbage's plan was to build something far more powerful.

Unfortunately, things didn't go smoothly. The money ran out in the 1830s, by which time Babbage had scrapped his first design anyway. It was only after this that he started work on his 'analytical engine'. This would have had most of the basic elements of a modern computer: instructions (from punched cards), a memory unit and a way of controlling the order of calculations. It was never finished.

Knowledge of Babbage's amazing machine was kept alive through a description by his friend **Ada Byron, Countess of Lovelace**, daughter of the poet Lord Byron, although his notebooks were only discovered in 1937. *Difference Engine No.2* was finally built from his notes by the Science Museum in London in 1991 - it is accurate to 31 digits.

In later life Babbage became rather odd: he campaigned against organ grinders, whom he hated with a deep, mad loathing, and, together with Ada Lovelace, he tried to invent a system for winning bets at horse races.

Henry, Joseph

He made magnets

1797-1878

Joseph Henry was the son of a American labourer. He escaped a life of drudgery due to the simple fact that he was brilliantly brainy. By 1829 he was experimenting with electromagnets. Until that time only weak electromagnets could be made, because the electric current in the coil kept jumping between wires, instead of running obediently around the coil - it kept short-circuiting in other words. Henry insulated the wire with silk from his wife's petticoats and thus made powerful electromagnets possible.

He also made very small magnets and thus helped invent the electric telegraph. An electromagnet can be switched on and off at a distance if it's attached to a long wire. The distant magnet can be made to pull a small iron bar towards it which will spring back if it's attached to a spring. This is the principle behind the very first telegraph. Since electricity can only travel so far down a wire before running out of steam, so to speak, due to electrical resistance, Henry invented the electrical relay to boost the current, so that messages could be sent over longer distances.

His greatest claim to fame is that he discovered electro-magnet induction (that a magnet can induce an electric current) in 1830, slightly before **Michael Faraday**. Faraday however published his results first and went on to invent the electric generator. Perhaps to console himself, Henry then invented the electric motor.

136

Goodyear, Charles

Inventor of vulcanised rubber

1800-60

A bad fairy must have been at the bedside when Charles Goodyear was born. He had bad luck by the bucketful. Most of his life was spent in debt. The bad luck started when he was quite young. He went into the hardware business with his father, an inventor of farmyard tools in Connecticut. Their company went bankrupt in 1830 and before long, Goodyear was in prison for debt.

He became interested in rubber in 1834, in fact he first experimented with it while in prison. Rubber was already being used for raincoats, but the trouble was that it went stiff in cold weather and sticky in hot weather. It was already known that sulphur stopped the stickiness, and Goodyear somehow managed to buy a process for treating rubber with sulphur. One day in 1839 he dropped a sulphur/rubber mixture on a hot stove and found that some of it had turned dry and bendable at the same time. He took out a patent* for the process of heating rubber with sulphur and called it after Vulcan the Roman god of fire - vulcanisation.

He never made money from his discovery, although not for want of trying. The process was too easy to copy. When he died, he was somewhere between $200,000 and $600,000 in debt. Vulcanised rubber is now used in many products, especially car tyres.

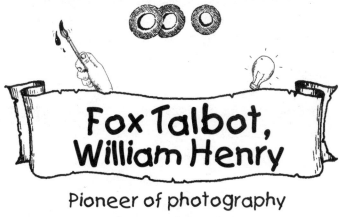

Fox Talbot, William Henry

Pioneer of photography
1800-77

One October's day in 1833, William Fox Talbot was sketching on the shores of Lake Como in Italy. He was using a type of pin-hole camera with a lense to project the image he wanted to sketch on to his paper, but without much success. He wasn't very good at drawing. It was then that he decided to draw using light itself as his pencil.

Fox Talbot was already interested in how light causes chemical reactions, and he probably knew of the work of **Joseph Niepce**, but he had no idea that the French artist, **Louis Daguerre**, was working in the same direction. He patented* his calotype process in 1841, shortly after Daguerre patented the Daguerrotype. To

116
133

make a calotype, the paper was first coated in silver chloride. It was exposed to light in a camera obscura, then the action of light on the silver chloride was exaggerated by washing in gallic acid - in other words, it was 'developed'. This negative image was then fixed so that light would have no more effect on it and positive photos could be printed from it.

A daguerrotype was a single positive image which couldn't be reproduced. It was Fox Talbot's invention of the photographic negative which paved the way towards modern photographic techniques. He continued to work on his invention, patenting the first photographic enlarger in 1843 and a method of taking instantaneous photos in 1851. Between 1844-6 he published a book of artistic photographs, the very first book to be photographically illustrated. *The Pencil of Nature* was what he'd set out to do that day on Lake Como.

Doppler, Christian Johann

He had an effect
1803-53

Imagine this nightmare: you're standing on a railway line and an express train is bearing down on you. Its whistle is screaming at you to get out of the way, you leap to the side just in time and the train rushes past, still screaming - phew!

If this happened in real life (don't try it, you might well end up dead), the pitch or note of the whistle would sound higher as it came towards you and lower as it moved away from you. This is because of the Doppler effect. Sound waves take on the speed of their source and the waves seem to be closer together when they come towards you and further apart as they move away. The distance between waves is what makes them sound higher or lower.

Doppler, an Austrian scientist, first described his effect in 1842. It was proved in Holland three years later in one of the maddest of all scientific experiments. For two days a trainload of trumpeters were driven up and down a length of railway track in a railway carriage blowing their hearts out to another group of musicians stationary on the ground. The stationary musicians, with their trained ears, could hear the change in pitch of the trumpet notes - as Doppler had said they would.

Doppler realised that the Doppler effect affects all wave motion, including light waves. The red shift of light happens when stars and galaxies are moving way from Earth. The wavelength of light coming from them appears to be longer and thus 'redder'. This has helped scientists to work out the size and age of the Universe.

Owen, Richard

Surgeon and dinosaur hunter

1804-92,

Richard Owen was an early dinosaur hunter (dinosaur bones, that is). It was Owen who coined the word 'dinosaur' meaning 'terrible lizard' (1842) and made the first large models of what dinosaurs might have looked like. His models were rather inaccurate, but they were put on show at the Crystal Palace in London in 1854. They fired the public interest in dinosaurs which continues to this day.

Owen's main interest was the dissection (cutting up) and classification of animals of different species*. He developed the system of classification started by **Cuvier**, became England's top zoologist and helped to set up the Natural History Museum.

Owen seems to have been jealous of **Charles Darwin's** fame. He fought biterly against Darwin's theory of 'evolution by natural selection', which is sad, because in 1859 when Darwin published his famous book, he and Owen had been friends for twenty years. In fairness, it wasn't evolution as such, which Owen objected to; it was evolution by natural selection. He believed that evolution happens through life forces within our cells*: a very woolly theory compared to Darwin's.

122

148

Brunel, Isambard Kingdom

Victorian engineer who built to last
1806-59

Isambard Brunel was a Victorian engineer. He's famous for his work on the Great Western Railway, especially for building the Royal Albert Bridge to carry trains across the Tamar, at Saltash in Plymouth, and for his ships. He understood that larger ships need less power per ton than smaller ships (this is because their surface area is smaller in relation to their total volume). The massive *Great Western*, built to his design, crossed the Atlantic four days faster than its rival the *Sirius* which was half its size. Following this, he built the *Great Britain*, the first large ship to be driven by screw propellers. It's now a museum in Bristol.

Brunel started by working on the first tunnel under the Thames, designed by his father, the inventor Marc Brunel. He was seriously injured when the tunnel flooded in 1828, and the design of the Clifton Suspension Bridge, his first major design, was completed while he was recovering from his injuries. It's still one of the most dramatic bridges in Britain.

Nasmyth, James

Inventor of the steam hammer

1808-90

James Nasmyth, a Scottish engineer, set up a workshop and foundry in Manchester in the 1830s. He's famous for inventing the steam hammer, a key tool of the Industrial Revolution used for forging. Forging is the process of hammering or pressing the hot metal to shape it and make it stronger. Massive, steam-powered hammers made it possible for the Victorians to hammer larger and stronger pieces of metal.

145 It came about in 1839, when **Isambard Brunel** asked Nasmyth to forge the shaft for the paddles which would propel his new iron ship, *Great Britain*. The steam hammer was Nasmyth's answer to the problem of forging this massive and vital component. From thought to finished sketch took just half an hour, which must make it one of the fastest inventions of all time. Brunel changed his mind and decided that the *Great Britain* would be powered by propellers instead of paddles, so Nasmyth never got to build his hammer. It was a man called Schneider, who built the first one in France, a direct copy from Nasmyth's sketch which he'd seen during a trip to England - Schneider also patented* the invention as if it was his own, in France. In 1842, Nasmyth saw the French hammer while on a return trip to France. He hurried back to England and built one of his own the same year - and patented it in England.

Braille, Louis

Inventor of Braille writing for the blind

1809-52

Louis Braille went blind when he was only three after an accident in his father's workshop. At ten he was sent to a school for blind children in Paris. There he learned a system called 'Night-Writing', developed by a certain Captain Charles Barbier for night-time messages on the battlefield. Aged only fifteen, Braille developed this into a system of reading and writing by touch for the blind.

In Barbier's Night-Writing the letters were printed in the form of groups or 'cells' of twelve raised dots on a flat surface such as cardboard. Braille's system was simpler with only six raised dots per cell. Depending on the position of the dots in each cell, sixty-three different 'letters' or numbers could be 'written'. The reader 'reads' Braille by passing his or her fingers lightly over the dots.

Braille has become standard all over the world. The only other system in fairly common use is Moon Type, invented by William Moon of Brighton in 1845. This uses the raised shape of normal letters and is easier to learn for people who go blind late in life.

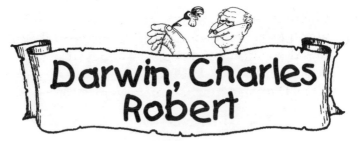

Darwin, Charles Robert

He put evolution on the map

1809-82

Before Charles Darwin published his famous book *On the Origin of Species by Means of Natural Selection* in 1858-9, most people still believed that God created all species* of living things at the beginning of the world. Lions had always looked like lions and gerbils had always looked like gerbils. Charles Darwin showed that species evolve gradually one from another, and God has nothing to do with it - at least not as described in the Bible.

Darwin was the son of a Shrewsbury doctor. In 1831 he joined a scientific expedition (1831-36) bound for South America, and the Pacific Ocean, on board the *Beagle*, as the ship's naturalist, a specialist in plants and animals. They sailed down the Atlantic coast of South America then up the Pacific coast. In the Galapagos Islands, far off the coast of Ecuador, Darwin saw how the same species of birds living cut off for centuries on different islands had developed in quite different ways. This and many other amazing discoveries led him to his theory of 'evolution by natural selection'.

His theory lies behind all modern ideas on how

different species of living things have come to be the way they are and how they will change in the future. It raised a storm of protest among religious leaders because it seemed to deny the story of creation in the Bible. Darwin's theory won out - and now he's buried in Westminster Abbey.

Otis, Elisha Graves

American inventor of the first safe lift

1811-61

Without lifts there could be no multi-storey modern buildings, and without a good safety device there would be no lifts safe enough for anyone sensible to get into. Elisha Otis designed the first safe lift and so made modern high-rise architecture possible.

Otis was a mechanic for a firm which made bedsteads. The firm decided to open a new factory, and Otis was put in charge of building operations. The new building was to have several floors connected by a hoist, but Otis was concerned for the safety of the workers. He knew of many accidents caused by failing hoists. He designed a safety device. Ratchets (a bit like the cogs in a cog wheel but straight, not set round a wheel) were installed in the sides of the shaft, and spring-loaded catches were attached to the hoist. They were attached in such a way that if ever the hoisting rope failed they would jam into the ratchets.

Otis patented* his invention in 1854 and went into business. He demonstrated it at an exhibition in New

York that same year, stepping into the lift himself and ordering a workman to cut the rope. Orders soon followed, and the first public passenger lift in New York was up and running by 1857. Like all early lifts it was powered by a steam engine. The age of sky scrapers had begun.

Simpson, James Young

Doctor who first used chloroform
1811-70

Early surgery was often more dangerous than the condition it was meant to cure. To have your leg sawn off with nothing but a bottle of gin to dull the pain was a horrific experience. Patients often died of shock.

General anaesthetics, used to make the patient go unconscious, were pioneered in America in the early nineteenth century and were a huge advance on gin. The chemicals used to produce unconsciousness were ether or nitrous oxide (laughing gas, discovered by 89 **Joseph Priestley**). James Simpson, a Scottish doctor and a pioneer of gynaecology (medicine to do with reproduction and childbirth in women), heard of the news from America in 1846. He experimented with ether almost immediately. Unfortunately, he found that it caused problems for some patients so he searched for something else which would do the trick. With two assistants he tried breathing chloroform. Next thing they knew they were underneath the table - they'd found the answer.

Some Christians claimed that it was wrong to dull the pain of childbirth because the pain was part of God's plan for women. Simpson pointed out that when God created Eve from Adam's rib, he put Adam to sleep first (the book of Genesis in the Bible). In 1853 he gave chloroform to Queen Victoria during the birth of her seventh child, Prince Leopold. Soon chloroform was being used by doctors all over the world for all kinds of surgery.

Bunsen, Robert Wilhelm

He liked a burner
1811-99

Bunsen burners are as common in chemists' laboratories as candles in cathedrals. The burner is a metal tube with holes in the bottom, which juts straight up from a workbench. Gas flows up the tube, drawing in air through the little holes. Gas and air burn together in a narrow flame at the top giving a steady heat for experiments. Wilhelm Bunsen, a German chemist, didn't invent the burner. He first used one in 1855 and was so keen on it that it's named after him anyway.

Bunsen was so dedicated to his work that he never married, saying he didn't have the time. He lost the sight in one eye due to a laboratory explosion, and he twice nearly poisoned himself while working on chemicals containing arsenic. His most important scientific discovery was to find that each chemical element* gives off light at its own particular wavelengths. This has been very useful to astronomers, since they have been able to find out what stars are made of by the light which shines from them.

Macmillan, Kirkpatrick

Inventor of the pedal bicycle

1813-78

The very first man-powered, two-wheeled vehicle was invented by Baron Karl de Drais in 1818. The rider simply scooted along the road by kicking against the ground on either side of a low seat. It was Kirkpatrick Macmillan, a Scottish blacksmith, who added pedals.

Macmillan built his improved version of a draisienne in 1839. The rider moved the pedals backwards and forwards rather than round and round, powering the back wheel by means of a system of rods and cranks. He used his invention to ride into Dumfries, his nearest town, but he never bothered to patent* it and never made any money out of it. In fact it never really caught on, perhaps because it weighed 25 kilograms. Nevertheless, Macmillan can reasonably claim to have invented the bicycle, if anything which has evolved from so many hands can ever be said to have been 'invented' at all.

Bessemer, Henry

He converted iron into steel
1813-98

In 1853 the Crimean War broke out. Russia was on one side, Britain, France and Turkey were on the other. It was a modern war where modern weapons did the killing. (It was in the Crimean War that the Light Brigade made its heroic but futile horseback charge against the Russian guns.) Henry Bessemer saw the need for yet more deadly weapons if the war was to be won. He invented a rotating shell for use by Britain and her allies. The British weren't interested but the French were - or would have been, if their cast-iron cannons had been strong enough to fire it. Bessemer decided to invent a process for making strong, cheap steel for use in cannons.

The trouble with cast iron is that it contains a lot of carbon and carbon makes it brittle. Until Bessemer came along, the carbon was removed by 'puddling', an expensive method of stirring and removing slag from molten cast iron to turn it into wrought iron. By 1856 Bessemer had discovered that blowing air through the molten cast iron burns off the carbon, in the process making the iron even hotter. Bessemer's converter was a special container lined with fire clay where the process took place. Cheap steel became available for the first time.

As well as his steel-making process, Bessemer invented a typesetting machine and methods for making lead pencils and gold paint. He also designed a massive 'swinging saloon' to stop sea-sickness on passenger ships, which wasn't a success.

Byron, Augusta Ada
Countess of Lovelace

The first computer programmer

1815-52

Ada Byron's parents separated two months after she was born. Her father, the famous poet Lord Byron, ('mad, bad and dangerous to know') had to leave the country because of the scandal. Little Ada never knew him and was brought up by her mother, the very clever Annabella Milbanke. Nevertheless she seems to have inherited her father's character. She grew up to be a fearless horse woman and a brilliant mathematician at a time when women mathematicians were very rare.

138 In 1833 she became interested in the work of **Charles Babbage** who had set out to build a calculating machine for the British government. Her notes on his invention are said to contain the world's first computer programme, although the main ideas may well have been Babbage's.

Ada and Babbage became friends. They worked together to design a system for winning bets at horse races. When she died of cancer in 1852, Ada was said to be thousands of pounds in debt due to gambling.

Joule, James Prescott

Energetic scientist who measured heat

1818-89

Energy is like an uninvited guest at a party. Tell him to go away and he comes back dressed as the vicar. Tell the vicar to go away and he comes back dressed up as the lady from number seven. Kill the lady from number seven and she comes back as the neighbour's dog! On the other hand, if he isn't there already and you ask him to come - he won't! This is all another way of saying that energy may take on different forms, such as heat or movement, but it can neither be created nor destroyed. This is the law of conservation of energy and is one of the most basic laws of science.

The joule, a unit of energy, is named after James Joule (4.18 joules are equal to 1 calorie of heat), the son of a rich Manchester brewer. Discovery of the relationship between heat and energy was his life's work. All his life he was obsessed with measuring things, from the temperature at the top and bottom of a waterfall (on his honeymoon) to the heat from the steam engine which he kept in his house in Manchester (despite the complaints of his neighbours). He discovered the Joule-

Thomson (later **Lord Kelvin**) effect, best tested by putting your finger over air escaping from a bicycle tube and feeling how cool it is. This is caused by the fact that gases cool when they expand - because they use up heat-energy in the process.

It was Joule who showed that heat is in fact a form of energy, and just one form among many. This discovery led later scientists to the law of conservation of energy - where we started. 'Joule's equivalent', commonly known as the 'mechanical equivalent of heat', helps scientists to calculate how much of one type of energy will convert into another.

Morton, William Thomas Green

American who etherised patients

1819-68

Ether is chemically similar to the alcohol in beer, wine or whisky. In liquid form it evaporates very easily, and it sends you unconscious if you breathe in the fumes. A handkerchief soaked in ether and placed under the nose is all it takes. In 1842 an American doctor called William Long removed a tumour from a patient who had first been made unconscious with ether. This was the first use of ether in surgery and the first experiment in modern anaesthetics. Before that time, just about all that could be done for a patient before an operation was to get him or her blind drunk.

Long wasn't interested in fame or wealth. It was William Morton, who patented* the use of ether in surgery and did most to publicise it. Morton was a dentist. He set up a practice in Boston in 1844 and became interested in ether after designing a new type of dental plate. Before the plate could be fitted into a patient's mouth, all remaining teeth had to be pulled out. A pretty drastic process - and very painful in those days. He took advice from his old teacher, a certain Charles Jackson, and in 1846 he administered ether before extracting the teeth of a patient. The patient didn't feel a thing (till afterwards anyway). That same year he held a public demonstration in which a facial tumour was removed under ether - and he patented the process. Jackson was included on the patent by way of payment for his advice. Unfortunately, this was the same Jackson who quarrelled with **Samuel Morse** about who invented the electric telegraph.

Perhaps Morton shouldn't have tried to claim ownership of the patent, after all he wasn't the real inventor. Be that as it may, he certainly paid the price for his greed. Jackson hounded him through the courts and claimed part of all the prizes awarded to Morton for the discovery. Morton died in poverty.

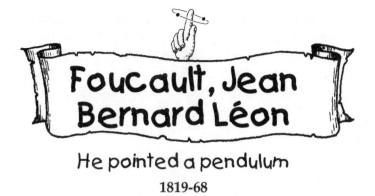

Foucault, Jean Bernard Léon

He pointed a pendulum

1819-68

Foucault started out as a doctor. Not a very good choice of job, since he couldn't bear the sight of blood. He became a scientist instead, and a very good one. He measured the speed of light in a clever experiment using mirrors. Other discoveries followed, but he's most famous for a dramatic experiment with a pendulum. 'Foucault's Pendulum' proved that the Earth is spinning.

It may seem strange, but although the idea that the Earth spins on its axis had first been thought of by an ancient Greek called Heracleides 2,200 years before, no one had thought of a way to prove it. Foucault's proof was based on the fact that a pendulum will tend to keep swinging along the line you first swing it in. So, if a really big pendulum swings for long enough, to anyone standing on 'solid' ground the line of the swing will seem to move - even though it's really the ground that's moving, because the Earth is rotating. At the north and south poles the pendulum will seem to move round in a complete circle every twenty-four hours.

With permission from Emperor Napoleon III, Foucault hung a large iron ball by a sixty-one metre steel wire from the dome of the Pantheon in Paris. A point jutting from beneath the ball was just long enough to trace a mark in sand scattered beneath. The ball was tied to a side-wall by a cord and to start the experiment the cord was cut by burning (so there would be no vibrations). The massive pendulum started to swing. The audience gasped - and waited. Lo and behold! 31 hours and 47 minutes later, the line of swing of the pendulum had changed direction in a complete circle - just as it should have done at that point on the Earth's surface.

Sholes, Christopher Latham

Inventor of the typewriter
1819-90

Christopher Sholes started his working life as apprentice to a printer. He rose to become a newspaper editor, a politician - and an inventor. In 1864 he patented* a device for automatically numbering pages. Shortly after, he heard of a recent plan for a writing device by a London inventor and it was suggested to him that the page numbering invention could be developed into an American machine for writing. No sooner said than done - well almost. It took him four years to complete the project and in 1868 he took out a patent on the world's first typewriter.

The first typewriter had many of the features of the modern version. The paper was rolled round a moving drum, there was a carriage return lever to move the drum back into position at the start of each line, line spacing and a mechanism that caused letter spacing by movement of the drum. The keys were moved by levers from a keyboard. The position of the characters on the keyboard hasn't changed from that day to this. It's called the QWERTY keyboard after the first six letters of the upper row. It's not an ideal arrangement, but we're stuck with it.

In 1873 Sholes sold his rights in the machine to a gunsmith by the name of Remington. Remington put the first commercial typewriter on the market in 1874.

Yale, Linus

Inventor of the Yale lock

1821-68

America in the nineteenth century was a lawless place. This was the age of gun-toting robbers who rode into town to hold up the local bank. In 1840 Linus Yale senior, father of Linus Yale, began to manufacture a pin and tumbler lock to help the banks fight back. This type of lock is often called the Egyptian lock because the same idea was widely used in Ancient Egypt more than 4,000 years ago. The ancient lock included a bar with holes cut into it, and a device of wooden pins crafted to fit the holes. The device was attached to the door and could be swung round to fall into the holes. The lock was a large wooden bar shaped like a toothbrush with pins to push out the pins of the lock. It was often carried on the shoulders.

Linus Yale junior tried his hand as an artist without much success, then decided to follow in his father's footsteps. In 1851 he designed the Yale Infallible Bank Lock and in 1862 the Yale Magic Bank Lock. But his great invention was the Yale cylinder lock with the small, flat serrated key, a variation on the pin and tumbler lock. It's still very widely used today.

Mendel, Gregor (Johann)

Monk with a mission who founded genetics*
1822-84

Johann Mendel spent most of his life in the Augustinian Abbey at Brünn in Austria. He became a monk in 1843, when he changed his name to Gregor. Mendel studied maths and science, but on the first three occasions he failed to pass the exams which would have qualified him to teach in high schools. He was especially bad at geology - and biology.

For eight years from 1857, while teaching science in a local school, Mendel researched plants. He worked in the small monastery garden, mainly with peas, crossing selected plants with each other, and carefully wrapping the flowers to avoid any accidental cross-pollination, so that he could be sure who the 'parents' were. He discovered that living things are not a blend of their parents' characteristics, all mushed together; they're a mixture of distinct bits and pieces.

To oversimplify, a red plant and a yellow plant don't produce a baby orange plant, they produce either a red or a yellow plant, depending on which characteristic is dominant. Each characteristic is inherited in a gene, half of which comes from each parent. The dominant half gives the characteristic, but the other half is still there so to speak, and may crop up in future generations. This discovery was vital to our understanding of evolution. **Darwin** had failed to iron out the one big weakness in his theory of evolution by natural selection - if inheritance was a simple matter of blending random characteristics, as Darwin had suggested, then even if nature selected something useful like claws for a cat, cats could easily blend back into a clawless mush within a few generations!

Mendel published his ideas in a local journal, but the value of his work wasn't understood. He became discouraged - and fat - and finally, an abbot. The discouragement meant that he didn't feel like carrying on with his work, the fatness meant that he couldn't bend down easily to tend to his peas - and being an abbot meant that he was too busy anyway. His discoveries were only recognised in the early 1900s, long after he was dead.

Pasteur, Louis

He gave us germs

1822-95

For most of history people have had no idea what really causes disease, although they've had their theories. The Anglo-Saxons, for instance, thought that disease was caused by nasty little elves armed with arrows. Louis Pasteur, a brilliant French chemist, abolished elves and other, more modern-sounding, but equally incorrect, theories for good. He discovered that many diseases are indeed caused by tiny living creatures (micro-organisms), not elves but *germs*. This was probably the most important of all medical discoveries. Without knowledge of the causes of disease it would be impossible for doctors to discover how to cure them.

Pasteur's interest in micro-organisms developed from his research into the problems of the French wine and vinegar industries in the 1850s. The problem was: how to stop the wine and vinegar going bad. Bad wine and vinegar cost the industry a lot of money. At that time many scientists believed that maggots and other horrid creatures arose from 'spontaneous generation' - that rotting meat, for instance, spawned maggots directly. Pasteur showed that wine and beer contain tiny yeast cells*, a type of micro-organism, and that the wrong type of yeast makes the drink go off - not the other way around. He invented pasteurisation (now used on milk). The liquid to be pasteurised is heated so that unwanted micro-organisms are killed.

Pasteur was then asked to look into the French silk industry, which was being ravaged by a disease of the silk worms. He discovered the germs which caused the epidemic, and his advice on how to defeat them saved the industry.

If micro-organisms could cause unpleasant results in drink, might they not do unpleasant things to living creatures - and to people? Following **Edward Jenner**, Pasteur developed vaccinations for anthrax in sheep and cholera in chickens. Most dramatically, he developed a vaccine for rabies, the deadly disease which is caught from the bite of a mad dog. In 1885 he treated a little boy who'd been savaged by a rabid dog and the little boy got better.

Pasteur became a good friend of the British doctor **Joseph Lister**. It was due to Pasteur's discoveries that Lister started antiseptic surgery, another life-saving breakthrough. Pasteur was made a member of the French Academy of medicine in 1873, although he'd never taken a degree in medicine.

Lenoir (Jean Joseph) Etienne

Frenchman who built the first internal combustion engine

1822-1900

The fire that powers a steam engine is kept separate from the water which it heats into the steam. It burns in its own tidy little chamber. Obviously, if the water got into the fire it would put it out. To burn fuel *inside* a cylinder and thus power the piston directly from the fire must have seemed like a pretty wild idea to people during the age of steam. Nevertheless, as early as 1824 the Frenchman Nicholas Carnot had written about it in an important book on heat.

In 1859, another Frenchman, Etienne Lenoir, built the first ever internal combustion engine. His machine had a separate storage battery which provided the spark to light the fuel/air mixture in the cylinder. It ran on coal gas, then used for lighting street lamps, and it was tough and reliable. Also it didn't need to build up a head of steam like a steam engine, and it was ready for work almost as soon as you started it. The main problem was that it was only 4% fuel efficient, which is horrific by modern standards.

Lenoir built a car powered by his engine in 1862. It took between two and six hours to cover just 9.6 kilometres (6 miles). His engines were more useful for powering small machines such as pumps or printing presses. By 1865, 400 were in operation in France and another 1000 in Britain. Some were still going strong twenty years later, having run continuously all that time. Despite his success, Lenoir died poor.

Thomson, William
Baron Kelvin of Largs

Scientist who started the kelvin scale

1824-1907

Molecules are like dancers at a specially energetic rave party, all frantically jigging about and banging into each other. William Thomson, the son of a mathematician from Belfast, is the scientist who realised that this movement energy of molecules is what we call heat. So when we measure temperature we're really measuring the movement of molecules. At -273.18° Celsius there's almost no movement at all. The dancers have all stopped for a drink. This temperature is known as absolute zero.

Baron Kelvin, as Thomson later became, invented a new scale for measuring temperatures which has proved to be very useful to scientists. In the Kelvin or absolute scale, 0° is absolute zero. Thereafter, each degree has the same value as a degree Celsius, so there are still 100° between the freezing and boiling points of water - between 273.18°K and 373.18°K.

Thomson gained a place at Glasgow University when only ten years old and his first paper, on mathematics, was read out at the Royal Society of Edinburgh. It was read out by an older man, because it didn't seem right that the learned professors of the Society should be lectured to by a schoolboy. Later he made a lot of money and bought himself a 126 ton yacht. By the end of his long career he too was a learned professor - and a lord.

Giffard, Henri

He designed the first airship

1825-82

The trouble with balloons is that they can't be steered. They've got less sense of purpose than a headless chicken. Off they go wherever the wind takes them. This makes them useful to travellers who don't care where they end up, but useless if you want to get to Paris in time for a football match.

Henri Giffard, a French engineer, designed the world's first ever steerable balloon, or 'airship'. It was forty-four metres long and filled with hydrogen. The propeller was powered by a steam engine and it was steered by a rudder which looked a bit like a sail. He called it a 'dirigible' from the French word *diriger*, to steer. It took off from the Paris Hippodrome on 24 September 1852 and flew for 30 kilometres (20 miles) at 10 kph (6 mph).

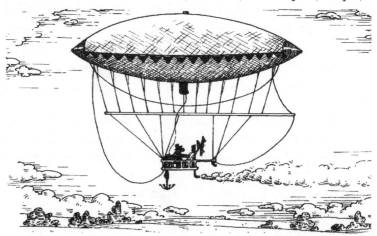

Lister, Joseph

Father of antiseptic surgery

1827-1912

In the mid-1800s no one was sure what caused wounds to get infected. One day they were clean, the next day they might be smelly and rotten. Old ideas about 'spontaneous generation', that maggots arose directly from mouldy meat for instance, were still widely believed. It wasn't until 1865 that the great French scientist **Louis Pasteur** discovered that diseases are caused by tiny living things, now called 'germs'.

164

To Joseph Lister, an English surgeon then working in the Glasgow Royal Infirmary, the importance of Pasteur's discovery was immediately obvious. If he could kill all the germs in the wounds of his patients during and after surgery, then there would no longer be any risk of infection by germs. To start with, he used carbolic acid as the most effective germ-killer - or 'antiseptic' as such germ-killers are properly called. He dressed wounds with carbolic, he soaked bandages in it, he even sprayed the air around an operation using a special carbolic spray. He then found ways of improving on pure carbolic.

The result: there were a lot less rotting wounds than there used to be, and deaths fell dramatically. Thanks to Joseph Lister, surgery would never be the same again.

Swan, Joseph Wilson

English inventor of the light bulb

1828-1914

Both carbon and metal are good candidates for 'best material with which to make an electric light filament'. Both conduct electricity. But there are two problems: metal wire melts if it gets too hot, carbon burns. If an electric current flows through either of them enough to produce light, then melting or burning is unavoidable.

Well not quite. Carbon won't burn in a vacuum. Nothing will. In 1845, twenty years before **Edison**, Joseph Swan connected filaments of burned paper, which is carbon based, to electric wires in a flask, then pumped out the air as best he could to make a vacuum. He sealed the flasks with corks to make the world's first electric light bulbs. Later he developed filaments made of cotton fibre.

It was very difficult to create a good vacuum until the invention of a vacuum pump in 1865, and it wasn't until 1880 that Swan was able to patent* his invention. Swan lamps became popular (the House of Commons was lit by them in 1881), but they weren't perfect. Among other things, there were problems with maintaining a steady flow of electricity as lamps were switched on and off. Meanwhile, the American inventor Edison had overcome many of these problems and had already invented his own cotton filament. In 1883 the two men joined forces and the Edison and Swan United Electric Light Company was formed.

Maxwell, James Clerk

Scotsman who fielded a force

1831-79

James Clerk Maxwell's 'field equations' aren't used to calculate the size of fields. They describe the relationships between electricity, magnetism and electro-magnetic radiation. Working at Cambridge in the years 1864-73, Maxwell described the laws of 136 **Faraday** in mathematical terms. Faraday had been a genius but a lousy mathematician. Maxwell proved beyond doubt what Faraday had suggested - that electricity and magnetism always exist together and that one can be used to produce the other, and vice versa.

But Maxwell saw a deeper pattern behind Faraday's findings. He showed that waves of radiation are given off when an electric current oscillates (repeatedly reverses its direction) - waves which travel outwards at the speed of light. He guessed (rightly as it turned out) that they are light itself. Therefore, Maxwell concluded, light itself is a form of electromagnetic radiation. Maxwell's field equations described a universe which is criss-crossed by an invisible web of electro-magnetic 212 fields and forces. Without Maxwell, **Einstein's** theory of 199 relativity and **Max Planck's** quantum theory would have been impossible - and there would have been no radio, no telephones and no television.

Maxwell also proved that heat is molecules jigging about at different speeds, not at the same speed. It had been thought by many scientists that the same types of molecules all move at the same speed at any particular temperature. Maxwell pointed out that this is impossible, since by bumping into each other some will slow down and others will speed up. 'Maxwell's demon' showed that heat need not necessarily spread out evenly through a gas.

Nobel, Alfred Bernhard

Discoverer of dynamite and giver of prizes

1833-96

Alfred Nobel's father invented an underwater explosive mine which was bought by the Russian government. Alfred worked in his father's Russian factory during the Crimean War (1853-56). When the war finished, demand for the mine fell off steeply and in 1859 the business went bankrupt.

Back in Sweden, father and son worked on ways to improve the explosive nitroglycerine (invented in 1846 by the Italian chemist Ascanio Sobrero) which has to be handled extremely carefully. Tragedy struck in 1864 when their little factory blew up, killing five people including his younger brother. Alfred set to work to make a safer explosive, on a barge in the middle of a lake to reduce the risk to others. It was there, in 1867, that he discovered dynamite, a mixture of nitroglycerine and a packing material. Unlike pure, liquid nitroglycerine it was solid and it was almost impossible to set off without a detonating cap. Later he invented an even safer form of the explosive, now commonly called gelignite. He also invented a smokeless gunpowder before **Hiram Maxim** invented cordite.

Alfred Nobel was a quiet man who never married. He became very rich due to his explosives factories and to ownership of oil wells in southern Russia. He seems to have believed that his inventions would make war so terrifying that war itself would become impossible. Fat hope. When he died, he left his money to fund five prizes: for literature, physics, chemistry, physiology and medicine - and peace. To win a Nobel Prize* is thought by many to be the highest honour in the world today.

Mendeleyev, Dmitri Ivanovitch

He tabled the elements

1834-1907

Mendeleyev had a disastrous start in life. His father, a teacher in Siberia, died soon after he was born, leaving his mother to care for him and his sixteen brothers and sisters. Soon after, the glass works run by his mother burnt down and they had to travel to St Petersberg, where Dmitri grew up to become a professor of chemistry. He never forgot the poverty of those early years and always travelled third class so as to keep in touch with ordinary people.

An element* is a chemical which can't be broken up into other chemicals (at least not by chemical reaction). In the early 1800s, **John Dalton** had worked out the atomic weights of several elements, while exploring his atomic theory of matter. Since then, several scientists had tried to list all the known elements according to their atomic weights and properties, hoping this would show what different groups had in common. Dmitri Mendeleyev

121

was by far the most successful of these scientists. His 'periodic table of the elements' is now a basic tool of chemistry.

From 1864-90 he was a professor at the Technical Institute of St Petersburg. It was during this period that he worked on his table of elements. He arranged them according to their atomic weights in such a way that elements having similar valences (the number of other elements with which they can combine) fell in the same columns. He discovered that there was a periodicity to the properties of the elements as they were laid out in his table (hence the name). What this means is that certain types of property cropped up at regular intervals as properties of different elements (for instance, conductivity of electricity). Mendeleyev could thus predict what properties an element might have, and he left gaps in the table for elements not yet discovered. This was laughed at at the time, but he was proved right within his lifetime by the discovery of three new elements exactly as predicted.

REACTIVE METALS · TRANSITION METALS · NON-METALS

PERIOD 1	H 1																	He 2
PERIOD 2	Li 3	Be 4											B 5	C 6	N 7	O 8	F 9	Ne 10
PERIOD 3	Na 11	Mg 12											Al 13	Si 14	P 15	S 16	Cl 17	Ar 18
PERIOD 4	K 19	Ca 20	Sc 21	Ti 22	V 23	Cr 24	Mn 25	Fe 26	Co 27	Ni 28	Cu 29	Zn 30	Ga 31	Ge 32	As 33	Se 34	Br 35	Kr 36
PERIOD 5	Rb 37	Sr 38	Y 39	Zr 40	Nb 41	Mo 42	Tc 43	Ru 44	Rh 45	Pd 46	Ag 47	Cd 48	In 49	Sn 50	Sb 51	Te 52	I 53	Xe 54
PERIOD 6	Cs 55	Ba 56	La 57	Hf 72	Ta 73	W 74	Re 75	Os 76	Ir 77	Pt 78	Au 79	Hg 80	Tl 81	Pb 82	Bi 83	Po 84	At 85	Rn 86
PERIOD 7	Fr 87	Ra 88	Ac 89	Ku 104	Ha 105													

Lanthanides/Actinides:

Ce 58	Pr 59	Nd 60	Pm 61	Sm 62	Eu 63	Gd 64	Tb 65	Dy 66	Ho 67	Er 68	Tm 69	Yb 70	Lu 71
Th 90	Pa 91	U 92	Np 93	Pu 94	Am 95	Cm 96	Bk 97	Cf 98	Es 99	Fm 100	Md 101	No 102	Lr 103

Mach, Ernst

Austrian who made shock waves

1838-1916

Mach numbers describe the speed of very fast objects. They're related to the speed of sound. The speed of sound varies. If sound travels through the air at a certain height on a certain day at 331.29 metres per second, then an aeroplane travelling at the same speed at the same time and place is said to be travelling at Mach 1. If the aeroplane travels at twice that speed it's travelling at Mach 2, and so on.

Ernst Mach published his research into air flow around moving objects in 1887. He also published photographs showing the shock waves around moving objects and was the first person to notice the dramatic change in the flow of air round an object as it reaches the speed of sound.

Mach thought it was very important to remember that scientific 'laws' are just ideas dreamed up by scientists. Only what we experience with our senses is reliable, according to Mach, and even that we have to be careful about. He refused to accept atomic theory because atoms can't be observed directly.

Zeppelin, Ferdinand
Count von Zeppelin

German who built an airship

1838-1917

Balloons are great, but they can only float where the wind blows them. An airship, or dirigible (directable, from the French *diriger*) balloon should, in theory, be more useful. The first airship was a 'blimp' or non-rigid, built by Frenchman **Henri Giffard** in 1852. It soon became clear that a rigid structure for the balloon would be stronger and more efficient. Count Zeppelin was the man who made a success of rigid airships.

Zeppelin was an army officer. His interest in flight began after an ascent in a balloon during the American Civil War (1861-65). In 1890 he retired from the German army and ten years later his first airship, the *LZ-1*, took off from a massive floating hangar on Lake Constance, on the southern border of Germany. It consisted of bags of hydrogen within a light metal frame and two engines, with a 'gondola' for passengers and crew hanging beneath.

Then in 1906 the German government ordered an entire fleet of 'zeppelins' and during World War I they flew many bombing missions over France and England. Being large and slow and full of inflammable hydrogen they weren't very successful. Forty were shot down. Safety was always a problem for airships, but by the 1930s, despite several disasters, there were regular flights across the Atlantic. Then in 1937, at Lakehurst New Jersey, *LZ-129*, the *Hindenburg*, exploded in flames while docking. It was the largest zeppelin ever built, a massive 245 metres long and it had a top speed of 135 kph (84 mph). Count Zeppelin had been dead for twenty years, but on that day his dream died, together with the thirty-six victims of the disaster.

Maxim, Hiram Stevens

Inventor of the automatic machine gun

1840-1916

Hiram Maxim was an American inventor who became a British citizen in 1900, having invented the Maxim gun in 1884. This was the first fully automatic machine gun. It could fire ten rounds a second from its water-cooled barrel and used the recoil from each shot to eject the used cartridge and to load and fire a fresh one. (The earlier Gatling gun had been hand powered.) The Maxim gun used cordite, a new smokeless explosive which Maxim also helped develop. For thirty years it helped the European powers in their colonial wars with less technologically advanced countries, giving rise to the rhyme:

Whatever happens we have got
The Maxim gun and they have not.

During World War I, which is sometimes called the 'machine gun war', the Maxim gun mowed down foot soldiers in their thousands. Maxim lived long enough to see this dreadful triumph.

As well as inventing the Maxim gun, he invented a range of other devices including patent* mousetraps and, in 1894, a steam powered aircraft which took off from rails. The water needed to make the steam was too heavy for the aircraft to work properly.

Dunlop, John Boyd

He tamed a tiresome tricycle
1840-1921

John Dunlop was a Scottish vet who set up practice in Ireland. It was there that he invented the first useful pneumatic tyre, a tyre filled with air.

It started in 1888 when his young son complained that the solid rubber tyres on his tricycle were uncomfortable. Dunlop designed an air-filled rubber hose to fit round the tricycle wheels, and Dunlop's son went on to win a tricycle race. Dunlop improved his design. His early tyres were air-filled rubber tubes held inside a linen 'jacket' with a rubber tread glued to the outside. Flaps from the 'jacket' bound the tyre to the wheel. The air was pumped in with a football pump.

Dunlop wasn't the first person to design a pneumatic or air-filled tyre. Another Scotsman, Robert Thomson, had patented* a design in 1845, but at that time rubber was still very expensive. Dunlop was in the right place at the right time. When he developed his tyre, the craze for cycles was well under way and motor cars would soon start to clutter the roads. Demand was enormous. He founded a company to produce the tyres. This company grew into the mighty modern company which still bears his name.

Dewar, James

Inventor of the thermos flask

1842-1923

Just as steam will turn from steam to water to ice depending on its temperature (and pressure), all other gases will also turn into liquids and then into solids if they're cold enough. James Dewar, a British scientist, was the first person to liquify hydrogen (1898) and the first person to freeze it a year later. It was while he was investigating how gases behave at very low temperatures that the idea of a thermos flask came to him. He invented his 'vacuum flask' in order to keep gases in a liquid state and at very low temperatures.

A thermos or vacuum flask has two walls with a vacuum between them - why it's also called a 'vacuum flask'.

Heat can't be conducted or convected across the vacuum because there's nothing there to conduct it or convect it. The only way for heat to escape or enter is by radiation and this is cut to a minimum by a silvery lining which reflects the heat back the way it came. What was designed for liquid hydrogen has turned out to be very useful on picnics.

Koch, (Heinrich Herman) Robert

Bacteria beater who drove out diseases

1843-1910

Consumption is a disease that poets die of, at least they're meant to. It makes them pale and interesting. In the later stages they may cough blood into a white handkerchief while lying on a couch. The great romantic poet John Keats is an example of this. The other name for this disease is *tuberculosis*, and, in reality of course, poets make up only a small number of its victims. It was one of the biggest killers of the nineteenth century.

Robert Koch was a German doctor. He studied bacteria*, tiny, single-celled* living things, which can cause diseases. He developed a reliable method of growing 'cultures' of disease-causing bacteria outside the human body in order to study them. Bacteria get everywhere given half a chance, and this had been a major headache for scientists. Koch grew his bacteria in solid gels (a bit like jelly) rather than liquids. Each type of bacteria was stuck in one place in its gel and so couldn't get mixed up with other types. He also developed methods of dying bacteria so that they were easier to see. In later life, an assistant, Julius Petri, developed a shallow, covered glass dish for growing bacteria. This type of dish, called a Petri dish, is used in laboratories all over the world.

164 Inspired by the great French scientist **Louis Pasteur,** Koch worked out the life cycle of the anthrax bacterium (1876). Anthrax is a disease which kills animals and can be passed to people. Six years later he found the bacterium which causes tuberculosis. Without his discovery, any scientific attempt at a cure would have been impossible, and because the disease was so common he became famous. He went on to discover the cause of cholera and that rats carry bubonic plague. Without his work there would be an awful lot more sick people than there are in the world today.

Benz, Karl (Friedrich)

He built the first practical petrol-driven car

1844-1929

The very first petrol-driven car was built by a Belgian
165 called **Jean Joseph Lenoir** back in 1859. It was a brilliant invention but incredibly inefficient. It drank petrol. So Karl Benz's petrol-driven car of 1885 wasn't the first petrol-driven car, but it was the first practical car.

Benz was just ahead of fellow German, Gottlieb Daimler, who built a four-wheel petrol-driven car in 1889. Benz's own car had been a three-wheeler, but two years later he followed up with a four-wheel version of his own. Meanwhile both men claimed to have invented the petrol-driven car, although neither of them had really. They became bitter rivals.

In 1926, in an unholy union, the companies of the two enemies teamed up to form Daimler-Benz. Daimler-Benz produced the first Mercedes-Benz. The 'Mercedes' bit was from a car already produced by Daimler, named after the daughter of one of his financial backers. The 'Benz' bit was of course named after Benz.

Röntgen, Wilhelm Konrad

Discoverer of X-rays
1845-1923

Ray guns may in future be used to zap alien invaders from outer space. In the meantime, they have a more humble use - there's a sort of ray gun at the back of every television set. The rays are cathode rays, a type of electron stream. Cathode rays make certain chemicals glow, which is why they're important in televisions. The cathode ray tube at the back of a television shoots rays on to the television screen at the front.

In 1895, Wilhelm Röntgen, was working with cathode rays at the University of Würzburg in Bavaria. One day, while he was aiming his cathode ray tube in one direction, a piece of chemical-coated paper in quite another direction started to glow. This was strange, because no way had it been hit by any cathode rays. He realised that rays of some strange, disobedient radiation had shone through the *sides* of the cathode ray tube at the same time as cathode rays were streaming obediently out of the front. Having no idea what on earth these new rays were, he called them X-rays, X being the letter normally used in maths to mean an unknown quantity. Working frantically over the next seven weeks, Röntgen discovered the basic nature of X-rays and showed that they can penetrate many substances which light cannot. At a public lecture later that year, he demonstrated an X-ray photograph of a human hand to wild applause.

Röntgen refused to patent* his discovery because he believed that the benefits of science should be available to everyone. At first, people didn't realise that X-rays must be treated with respect because they can cause cancer. X-rays even became a fairground attraction. Röntgen's discovery led to a frenzy of scientific
190 experimentation. Within months **Becquerel** had discovered radioactivity and the atomic age had begun.

Westinghouse, George

American who drove the DC from AC/DC

1846-1914

George Westinghouse was the son of an agricultural tools manufacturer. He ran away from school when he was fifteen to fight in the American civil war on the side of the Yankees. Soon after his return home he started his career as an inventor. By the age of nineteen he'd applied for the first of more than four hundred patents*.

The invention which made his fortune was an air brake for trains, which he patented in 1869. His brake was so safe that in 1893 air brakes were made compulsory on all American trains. He made a fortune.

In 1880 Westinghouse decided to go into electricity generation and developed an efficient means of delivering alternating current (AC). AC current constantly changes its direction of flow. (The standard rate of change in modern America is sixty times a second, in Britain it's fifty.) The big advantage of AC is that voltage can be raised very high with a transformer before delivery along high-voltage lines. This greatly reduces loss of power during transmission compared to direct current (DC). AC can then be reduced down to a safer level before delivery to the end user.

In America the struggle between the supporters of AC,

led by Westinghouse, and DC, led by **Edison**, was hard and bitter. Both had invested large sums of money in their own systems. DC supporters claimed that AC was dangerous to human life. They even arranged that a Westinghouse AC generator should be the official generator for executions by electric chair in New York state, and they coined the word 'Westinghoused' for execution by this method. To no avail. The advantages of AC were too great and Westinghouse won the day.

Bell, Alexander Graham

Inventor of the telephone
1847-1922

Alexander Bell's first interest was in helping the deaf to speak. This was a family tradition. His father also taught speech to the deaf. In 1870 the family moved from Scotland to Canada and soon after, Bell opened a school for the training of teachers to the deaf.

He began to look for a way to make artificial speech using electricity, as such a device would be useful to very deaf people. One of his pupils, a young mechanic called Thomas Watson helped him, and the parents of two other pupils provided the money. It then occurred to Bell that by converting sound vibrations into electric current and then converting them back to sound at the other end of an electric wire, speech could be made to travel long distances. One day, while working on a version of this idea, he spilt battery acid on his trousers and called out to Watson: 'Watson, come here. I want you!'. Watson heard his words - over the line. It was the very first telephone call.

Bell patented* his invention in 1876 and formed the Bell Telephone Company. Soon there were telephones all over the place. Queen Victoria had one by 1877. Nothing could stop Bell now. Here are just *some* of the other things he invented: an improvement on **Edison's** gramophone, a hydrofoil boat which could go faster than 112 kph (70 mph), flat-disc records, an air cooling system, a method of taking salt from sea water, a forerunner of the iron lung, and a kite which could carry a man. Oh, and he also helped to start the *National Geographic* magazine.

Edison, Thomas Alva

Inventor of a lot of things
1847-1931

Thomas Alva Edison is probably the greatest inventor the world has ever known. In 1876, when he set up the world's first industrial research laboratory in New Jersey (an invention factory in all but name), his plan was to invent something new every ten days. By the end of his life he'd patented, either alone or with others, 1,093 inventions, far more than anybody else before or since.

Not that his Michigan teacher thought he was anything

special. He told Edison's mother that the boy was 'addled' - perhaps because Edison was half deaf. Mrs Edison knew better. She took him out of school and taught him herself. He had an amazing memory and could remember almost everything he read - and he read at an amazing speed, racing through the pages nearly as fast as he could turn them.

He patented* his first invention in 1868, an electrical vote recorder for the House of Congress. Other inventions followed thick and fast. The greatest are the electric light bulb (for which he shares the credit with British scientist, **Joseph Swan**), an efficient electric generator, several devices which pretty well started the cinema industry, the first phonograph (the ancestor of the record player) and the first commercial power distribution system.

Edison claimed that genius is '1% inspiration and 99% perspiration'. He worked about as hard as it's possible for a human being to work. His average working day was twenty hours, broken up by the odd snooze when he was exhausted. He became the most famous American of his day, the ultimate rags to riches story of the American dream.

Lilienthal, Otto

German engineer who flew to fame

1848-96

By 1890 a number of people were trying to fly by means other than by balloon, which was the only available method until then. Lilienthal was the most important of these pioneers. He studied the flight of birds, experimenting with flying models, some of which flapped their wings and some of which didn't. And he wrote a book, *Flight of Birds as the Basis of the Act of Flying*, which was widely read. It was Lilienthal who first saw the importance of cambered wings (which he modelled on birds' wings). Cambered wings are curved on the upper surface. This makes air flow more swiftly above the wing than below it, forcing the wing upwards.

From 1891, Lilienthal flew around two thousand test glides from an artificial hill near Lichterfelde in Germany, trying out both biplane and monoplane gliders. By that time he'd realized that wings which flap aren't the answer. The pilot hung beneath the wings as in a modern hang glider. He died of injuries after a crash while testing the design for a new rudder. Seven and a half years later, the **208** **Wright** brothers made the first powered flight, using many of Lilienthal's ideas.

Becquerel, (Antoine) Henri

Frenchman who discovered radioactivity

1852-1908

Fluorescent materials give off light for a while if they're first bombarded by radiation. The radiation can be light itself. That's why a fluorescent clock glows in the dark but has to be left out in the light first. Henri Becquerel wondered if fluorescent materials give off other types of radiation as well as light, such as X-rays for instance.

In 1896 he wrapped a photographic plate in black paper and put it in the sunshine with a lump of fluorescent material on top of it. Light wouldn't get to the photographic plate through the black paper, but if the fluorescent material gave off X-rays, the X-rays would. X-rays will get through almost anything, which is why we use them to take pictures of our bones.

As he expected, the photographic plate was fogged when he developed it. He was impatient to repeat his experiment, but the next few days were cloudy. To fill the time, he developed a photographic plate which he'd kept wrapped, but which had been stored near a lump of his fluorescent material in a drawer - strangely, *that* photographic plate was also fogged, seriously fogged. This was really odd. It meant that the radiation from the fluorescent material which had caused the fogging had nothing to do with sunlight, because the fluorescent material hadn't been exposed to sunlight while in its drawer. Radiation was coming from the material itself - which happened to contain uranium. Two years later the famous scientist **Marie Curie** called this strange new phenomenon 'radioactivity'.

Ehrlich, Paul

Doctor who made a difference
1854-1915

Paul Ehrlich, a brilliant German-Jewish bacteriologist, developed *immunology*. Immunology uses the natural defences of living cells* to zap disease-causing bugs. He then founded *chemotherapy*. Chemotherapy uses chemicals to zap the bugs.

Ehrlich discovered that living cells have 'side-chains' which stick out from the main body of each cell. These 'chains' absorb food chemicals, but they also absorb toxins, poisons which are given off by enemy, disease-causing bacteria*. Once a cell has absorbed a toxin from an enemy bacterium, it tends to grow lots of new side-chains, provided it's still alive. These new chains defend it against any more doses of the toxin - the cell can't be poisoned any more. It has become *immune* to the bacterium. In 1894 Ehrlich used an anti-toxic serum grown from immune cells in the blood of horses to cure children of the deadly childhood disease diphtheria.

However, many diseases can't be cured by serums. This was why Ehrlich set to work to find chemicals which might do the job even better. These chemicals, or 'magic bullets' as he called them, would have to poison diseased cells but leave the rest of the body alone. In 1909 he discovered Salvarsan, a chemical cure for the deadly disease, syphilis. Chemotherapy was on its way.

Parsons, Charles Algernon

English inventor of the steam turbine
1854-1931

Pity the poor piston. If pistons could think, they would get horribly bored. All that ever happens to them is that they get driven up and down a cylinder.

There's a limit to what you can do with an up and down movement. It has to be converted into a circular movement before the engine can drive a wheel or wheels. In a standard steam engine, the change-over to circular movement is done by means of mechanical couplings, and energy is used up in the process. How much more efficient if the steam can be made to drive a circular movement directly.

The idea of powering a circular motion directly from steam was already in the air in the 1880s when Charles Parsons started to study the problem. In 1884 he built the world's first useful steam turbine, in which a jet of high-pressure steam played directly on to the blades of a wheel inside a cylinder. He opened a turbine factory in

Newcastle in 1889 and went on to experiment with turbine-powered ships. At the Diamond Jubilee of Queen Victoria in 1897 his ship *Turbinia* steamed effortlessly past the massed ranks of the ships of the Royal Navy at 34.5 knots, an incredible speed at the time. A naval ship tried to catch the cheeky intruder, but couldn't. After this unofficial advertisement, orders for engines for turbine-powered warships and merchant ships flowed in.

The steam turbine was even more useful for generating electricity than it was for powering ships. The whirling, circular wheel of the turbine is perfect for driving a massive alternator of the type first discovered by
136 **Faraday**. Parsons' turbines generate most of the electricity in Britain and throughout the world.

Eastman, George

He rolled out Box Brownies

1854-1932

Before George Eastman came along, photographers needed a whole laboratory of stuff to prepare and develop their photographs. It was expensive, and you almost had to be a chemist as well as a photographer to do it properly. Eastman's company slogan was quite a contrast. It said: 'You press the button, we do the rest.'

Eastman became interested in photography in 1877 while working in Rochester, New York, where he was brought up. He experimented with various techniques, and by 1880 he'd invented a method of making dry photographic plates which could be carried with the photographer. Before that, photographers had to prepare wet plates on the spot before taking a photograph. Four years later he invented flexible paper film.

The first Eastman box cameras were sold in 1888. They came complete with a film of 100 shots. When the film was used up, the whole camera, film and all, went back to the factory for development and reloading. Before long, the paper film was replaced with a roll of transparent film (which lead to the invention of 'movies'). In 1900 he produced his first 'Box Brownie', a simple camera which sold for a dollar.

Eastman got seriously rich, but he came from a poor family and riches never spoiled him. He always cared for his workers, and in 1924 he gave away half his huge fortune. He killed himself in the end, rather than face his remaining years alone.

Gillette, King Camp

He gave cut-throats competition

1855-1932

Before Gillette came along, men had two choices: either use a cut-throat razor (a razor with an unguarded blade) or grow a beard. Some sensibly grew beards, but a lot thought they looked better clean-shaven. Cut-throats were hard to use, as their name implies, and they had to be sharpened on a leather strap.

When Gillette was sixteen, his family lost everything in a fire in Chicago and he went to work as a travelling hardware salesman. It was the boss of a hardware company who advised him to invent 'something that would be used and thrown away' - so the customer would come back for more. Gillette hit on the idea of a slim metal blade held in place between two protective metal plates - and the safety razor was born. His company was founded in 1903. He became extremely wealthy.

Thomson, Joseph John

Discoverer of electrons and supporter of plum pudding

1856-1940

During the 1890s, scientists disagreed about cathode rays, the rays which appear when an electric current passes through a near vacuum. Some said cathode rays were waves in the ether, a weightless stuff which was thought to fill all empty space. Others said that they were streams of tiny particles. In 1897, Joseph Thomson proved that the followers of the particle theory were right: cathode rays were indeed streams of tiny particles - very tiny indeed. In fact, they were smaller than atoms of hydrogen, the smallest of all atoms. He called his tiny particles 'corpuscles' but they soon became known as electrons. They were the very first sub-atomic particles to be discovered.

As a result of his work with electrons, Thomson became a firm believer in the plum pudding theory of atoms - that atoms are round balls of positive electrical charge with little plums of negative electrons stuck in them to neutralise them. The poor old plum pudding didn't last long. From 1884-1919, Thomson was director of the Cavendish Laboratory at Cambridge and the brilliant young New Zealander, **Ernest Rutherford**, worked under him from 1895. By 1906 Rutherford had suggested the structure of the atom still agreed on today, where electrons whizz in empty space around the atomic nucleus. Not that Thomson minded. He was

206

a brilliant teacher. Seven of his ex-students got Nobel prizes* and, due to his work at the Cavendish Laboratory, England led the field in sub-atomic physics for a generation.

Hertz, Heinrich Rudolf

Discoverer of radio waves
1857-94

Imagine that an electric spark is a trapeze artist high up at the top of a circus tent. Every time she swings from one platform to the other she throws out a handful of glitter. It floats away from her in a beautiful, expanding ring, out and out towards the sides of the tent. The slower she swings from one platform to the other, the greater will be the distance between one ring of glitter and the next.

Now imagine that the trapeze artist is a spark once more, oscillating backwards and forwards between two poles. The expanding rings of glitter are now waves of electromagnetic radiation. In 1883 Heinrich Hertz, a German professor of physics, measured electromagnetic waves which he had created from a spark of electricity which oscillates between two metal balls.

Light, which is also electromagnetic radiation, travels at 299,728 kilometres per second (186,282 miles). That means that if each light wave starts out from its source one thousandth of a second after the one in front, then each wave will be an enormous 299 kilometres (186 miles) long. So Hertz expected that his waves would be very long indeed. In actual fact they were 66 cm long - which is still a million times longer than the wave length of visible light.

210 In 1894 the brilliant Italian inventor **Guglielmo Marconi** developed a method for sending and receiving long 'Hertzian waves' as a means of communication without wire. Hertzian waves became known as 'radio waves'. Radio is short for *radiotelegraphy*, that is: telegraphy by radiation - telegraphy without wires. Sadly, Hertz died of blood poisoning at the young age of thirty-six, so he never lived to see the full results of his discovery.

Diesel, Rudolf Christian Karl

He developed the diesel engine

1858-1913

Diesel became interested in the internal combustion engine while working as manager of a German ice factory. He experimented with different types of fuel, including coal dust, before he invented the Diesel engine as we know it today. Unlike the standard petrol engine, Diesel's engine doesn't use a spark to light the fuel in the cylinder, instead it uses heat caused by compressing the air in the cylinder before the fuel is injected into it. Diesel engines are very efficient and diesel fuel is a heavier, safer type of petroleum than the petrol used in normal car engines. The only trouble is that diesel fuel freezes in very cold weather and diesel engines are bigger and heavier than petrol engines. However, they're perfect for large machines like trucks and ships. Nowadays some of them are light enough to be used in cars.

Diesel made a lot of money out of his invention. In 1913, he disappeared from the deck of the mail steamer *Dresden*. It's thought that he fell into the sea. He may have committed suicide.

Planck, Max Karl Ernst

He quantified quantities of quanta

1858-1947

Max Planck was a German scientist who laid the foundation stone of what's now called 'modern' science, as opposed to the classical science, practised since **Isaac Newton's** day.

67

From 1889-1926, Planck, a professor at the University of Berlin, was interested in 'black body' radiation. An object which absorbs all the light which shines on it (thus a 'black body') should in theory radiate all frequencies of light when it's heated up - but it doesn't. It glows orange first then yellow, through red hot to white/violet hot like an electric fire.

Which doesn't make sense, or at least it didn't until Planck came along. This takes us to the 'violet catastrophe'. Just as there are infinitely more numbers higher than say a hundred, or a million come to that, so there are infinitely more frequencies of light higher than orange, which is at the low frequency end of the spectrum. This means that the light given off by a heated black body should be very, very violet, the highest frequency visible light - the 'violet catastrophe'. Planck suggested that the reason there is no violet catastrophe is because energy is radiated in little bundles. He called the little bundles 'quanta'. Low frequency quanta need less energy to get started than high frequency ones, so the chances of them forming are higher and there are more of them than there ought to be (if all things were equal so to speak). The relationship between frequency of radiation and size of quantum is known as 'Planck's constant'. Like the speed of light, it's one of the most basic facts of the Universe.

In 1930 Planck became President of the Kaiser Wilhelm Society of Berlin which was renamed the Max Planck Society. He lived on to resist Hitler and the Nazis as best he could, but suffered the sadness of losing his first wife and all their four children. His youngest boy was killed by the Nazis after a failed assassination attempt on Hitler.

Arrhenius, Svante (August)

Scientist who 'discovered' global warming and that atoms are more than lumps.

1859-1927

136 From at least the time of **Faraday** many scientists thought that electric current was the movement of tiny particles. Faraday had studied the flow of current through liquid solutions. He called the particles which carried the current through a liquid 'ions', from the Greek word for a wanderer.

Svante Arrhenius, a Swedish chemist, studied how electric current passes through certain liquid solutions, electrolytes as Faraday called them, and not through others. He didn't find out exactly what an electric current *is*, but he did discover that atoms themselves can carry an electric charge - or not, as the case may be - and that this electrical charge can change. This was a lot more important than it sounds. It meant that atoms were no longer basic lumps of stuff which couldn't be broken up, as was thought at the time. Arrhenius was given the lowest possible pass for describing this absurd theory in his doctoral thesis of 1884. But during the next ten years he was proved right with the discovery of
196 electrons by **Joseph Thomson** and of radioactivity by
190 **Henri Becquerel**. Ion is now the name given to an electrically charged atom or group of atoms.

In later life Arrhenius suggested that burning too many

fossil fuels such as oil and gas would lead to a build-up of carbon dioxide into the air, trapping heat and causing global warming. He also suggested that spores of life drift through space on tides of radiation and that life occurs whenever the spores land on fertile soil - such as Earth.

Baekeland, Leo Hendrik

He made plastic

1863-1944

Leo Baekeland was a brilliant Belgian chemist. In 1889 he moved to America where he invented the first commercial photographic paper. He set up a company 193 to manufacture it and sold out to **George Eastman** in 1899 for a million dollars.

At that time the electricity industry was still young. Shellac was often used as an insulator. Shellac comes from a substance called lac, produced by Lacifer lacca, an insect from south-east Asia. It was quite expensive. In 1905 Baekeland set out to find something cheaper. He came up with a mixture of phenol and formaldehyde (used for preserving dead things) formed under pressure and heat. Bakelite was announced to the waiting world in 1909. It was the first commercially useful plastic because it didn't go soft when heated. Baekeland made another fortune.

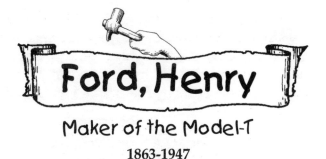

Ford, Henry

Maker of the Model-T

1863-1947

Henry Ford was the first car maker to mass-produce cars. Nearly 17 million Model-T Fords were sold from 1908-27.

A farm boy from Michigan, Ford built his first car in 1896, the Quadricycle, so called because is ran on four bicycle wheels. His most famous car, the Model-T, was a cheap car for everyday people. (He named his cars alphabetically, but not logically - they went A, B, C, F, K, N, R, S, T and A again.) To keep costs to a minimum, his workers stood at 'assembly lines' which brought the pieces to the workers rather than the other way around. While other manufacturers took up to twelve hours to build a chassis, Ford got this down to 93 minutes. By the end he was building a complete car every 24 seconds. Prices tumbled.

However, delays were caused by the wait for parts and raw materials from outside the factory. To avoid these delays, Ford bought mines, forests, even glass-making factories. Iron ore from his mines would arrive at his foundries, be turned into metal and sent to the assembly line. Within twenty-eight hours of arriving, the raw rock came out the other end as a car.

To start with, Ford payed his workers twice what he had to but this didn't last. When he retired in 1945 his company was worth a massive $1 billion - a huge sum in those days.

The Lumière brothers
Auguste and Louis

Pioneer of cinema

Auguste 1862-1954, Louis 1864-1948

Louis Lumière and his brother Auguste were the sons of a painter, Antoine Lumière, who opened a photographic studio in Lyon. They were both very clever. Louis invented a reliable method for making photographic plates, and the family opened a factory. By 1894 they were manufacturing fifteen million photographic plates a year.

187 That same year their father saw **Edison**'s Kinetoscope in Paris and told his sons about it. Only one viewer at a time could peer into Edison's Kinetoscope and see the small moving image. The Lumières took from Edison the idea of moving the strip of film forward by means of sprockets down the edge, powered by little cog wheels, but they combined this with an idea of a French inventor, Emile Reynaud, for projecting still pictures on to a big screen. The result was the Cinématographe, the world's first movie projector (where the word 'cinema' comes from). The Cinématographe ran at sixteen frames per second, slower than the standard modern speed of twenty-four frames per second. It was shown to the

public in a Paris café on 28 December 1895, and within months there were Cinématographes all over Europe. The first ever movie was *La Sortie des Ouvriers de l'usine Lumière* (Workers leaving the Lumière factory). The brothers went on to make the first movie comedy and the first news reels and documentaries. They also opened the world's first cinema.

Curie, Marie

Discoverer of polonium and radium

1867-1934

Uranium is dangerously radioactive, but it's mild as milk compared to some other radioactive elements*. Marie Curie and her husband, the French scientist Pierre Curie, discovered something far more powerful.

During the 1890s Marie Sklodowska was a poor young Polish scientist working in Paris. Her imagination had been fired by the recent discoveries of X-rays by **Röntgen** 183 and of the radioactivity (named by Marie) of uranium by **Becquerel** 190. After she married Pierre in 1895 the young couple started their own investigations into uranium. Pierre gave up his own work to be her helper. He was right to do so: she was perhaps the greatest woman scientist of all time.

They extracted their uranium from a mining ore called pitchblende. But it soon became clear that this ore gave off a massive amount of radiation, far more than could possibly be produced by uranium alone. Mary realised that another material must also be radiating, and far more powerfully. She and Pierre set to work. They laboured for four years in a leaky old shed in Paris, and from a vast quantity of pitchblende (8 tons) they extracted just one gram of radium chloride. This was the source of the additional radiation. The radium was *two million times* more radioactive than uranium. Here was a racehorse indeed.

In all, the Curies discovered two new elements: radium and polonium, called after Marie's native Poland. They worked closely together until Pierre was run over by a horse-drawn cart in 1906. Marie kept on working until she died of leukaemia caused by radioactivity. Her notebooks are still so radioactive that they can't be touched without protective clothing.

Rutherford, Ernest

Scientist who saw inside the atom
1871-1937

Elements* are the building bricks of the Universe. They join together to make simple molecules such as water (a compound of atoms of the elments, hydrogen and oxygen) and horribly complicated molecules such as DNA, the code of life itself. Molecules can split into the atoms of elements and thus form new substances, but there's nothing that can change an element itself.

At least that's what scientists used to think. Then
¹⁹⁰ radioactivity was discovered by **Becquerel** and the
²⁰⁵ **Curies** and it was now possible to look into the guts of
atoms. Suddenly elements weren't quite as 'elemental'
as they had seemed before. Ernest Rutherford, from
New Zealand, was the greatest scientist of the
revolution which followed. He started in 1895, hot on
the heels of the Curies. His great discovery was the
atomic nucleus. Rutherford fired sub-atomic particles
through gold foil which was so thin that it was only

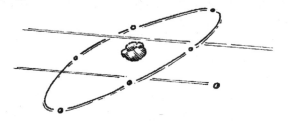

2,000 atoms thick - so thin that most of the sub-atomic
particles passed straight through it. This proved that
most of the gold was actually empty space. However,
some of the sub-atomic particles bounced right back the
way they'd come. This showed that scattered through
the almost empty space of the gold foil there must be
the tiny but heavy *nuclei* of atoms of gold. Rutherford
had proved that atoms have a tiny but heavy, nucleus
surrounded by lots of empty space with electrons
whizzing around inside.

Rutherford then suggested that the positive electric
charge of the nucleus is equalled by the negative charge
of the electrons and that the nucleus is partly made of
positive particles which he called protons.

He also suggested that radioactive decay happens when
sub-atomic particles escape from the nucleus. 'Half-life'

was his name for the time it takes for one type of atomic nucleus to decay into another. If the nucleus could change, that meant that the fundamental nature of the atom could change - that it could even become a different element. In 1919 he became the first person to change one element into another artificially when he split atoms of nitrogen into atoms of oxygen and hydrogen.

The Wright brothers
Wilbur and Orville

They built the first aeroplane
Wilbur 1867-1912, Orville 1871-1948

Wilbur and Orville Wright were the sons of an American minister. Like their father they were very proper, so proper that they usually wore suits even in their workshop. They never drank, never smoked and never got married. They were also designers and inventors of genius.

At first they built bicycles and printing presses. (Orville was a champion cyclist and they ran a bicycle shop.) 189 Then they became interested in gliding. After **Otto Lilienthal** died in 1896, they decided to build a powered aircraft. This was a huge undertaking since much of the necessary technology wasn't invented. By 1899 they'd flown a kite to test their invention of 'wing-warping', a method of steering by twisting the wings, the ancestor of modern ailerons. They tested more than a hundred different wing designs in a wind tunnel, also their own invention. They also designed a light but powerful engine. By 1903, after many trials with test gliders, they were ready for their first powered flight. On 17 December 1903, on Kill Devil Hills, near Kitty Hawk in North Carolina, Orville Wright flew 36.6 metres in 12 seconds. The first ever aeroplane flight. By the end of that momentous day, Wilbur had flown 260 metres in 59 seconds.

Only five other people saw those first flights and there was surprisingly little interest. In 1905 the Wrights offered their invention to the US War department but were turned down. Success came when they demonstrated their invention in Europe in 1908-9. Unfortunately, Wilbur didn't have many years left to enjoy his fame. He died of typhoid in 1912. Orville sold out of their company soon after, although he lived on for many years, one of the most famous and honoured men in America.

Marconi, Guglielmo

Italian pioneer of radio

1874-1937

Guglielmo Marconi read about the discoveries of 197 **Heinrich Hertz** in 1894. He immediately started to wonder how the new hertzian waves (now called radio waves) could be put to use. Using a coherer (a packet of loose metal filings which conduct extra current when bombarded with radio waves), the waves could be made to create electrical signals, and the electrical signals can be converted into sound - a radio message in fact. He began to experiment with methods of transmitting and receiving. By 1895 he'd sent a message from his house to his garden and later that year he sent one over a distance of more than a mile.

Marconi was Italian, but the Italian government of the time weren't interested in his work. Fortunately his mother was Irish, so he spoke English as well as Italian. He took himself off to England. There, with the help of the chief engineer of the Post Office, he sent a signal over nine miles. He formed the Wireless Telegraph and Signal Company Ltd (later Marconi's Wireless Telegraph Company Ltd) and took out an English patent* on his invention.

Over the following years he steadily increased the distance of his transmissions, experimenting with different types of aerial and transmitter. Perhaps his greatest triumph came in 1901. It was commonly expected that radio signals could travel no further than the horizon, but Marconi was confident that they would follow the curvature of the Earth. (It was not then known that this is due to them being reflected off the upper atmosphere.) Using aerials suspended from balloons he sent a signal from Cornwall, England across the Atlantic to Newfoundland, USA. In 1918 he sent a signal right the way round the world from England to Australia.

Marconi became very wealthy but rather than relaxing with his wealth, he kept trying out new ideas. He had a laboratory on board his yacht *Electra*. It was on *Electra* that he started to experiment with short-wave radio, which became the standard for long distance radio.

Meitner, Lise

She helped split the atom

1878-1968

215 Lise Meitner worked in Berlin with **Otto Hahn**. They were friends for thirty years, working together at the Kaiser Wilhelm Institute for Chemistry. Being a woman, her work was made absurdly difficult - she wasn't allowed into laboratories if any men were working in them at the time. Eventually, she and Hahn set up their own separate laboratory in a carpenter's workshop.

And somehow, despite this nonsense, she was made joint director of the Institute in 1917.

Meitner was an Austrian Jew. Being an Austrian and therefore a foreigner, she was safe after the Nazis took power in Germany - until 1938, when they took over Austria and started to kill Austrian Jews. Then she fled, working first in Stockholm and then at Cambridge. Meanwhile, Hahn sent her the results of some very interesting experiments. He had bombarded uranium, which is very heavy, with neutrons - tiny, neutral, sub-atomic particles. Some of the uranium had turned into barium which is a far lighter element*. Hahn hesitated to believe the evidence of his eyes, but Meitner was certain: the nuclei of the uranium atoms had split in two. Hahn had split the atom. In 1939, she published her thoughts on Hahn's results, calling the process 'nuclear fission'.

It was nuclear fission which made the atom bomb possible, but Meitner never worked on it. She lived till ninety - three months longer than her old friend Otto.

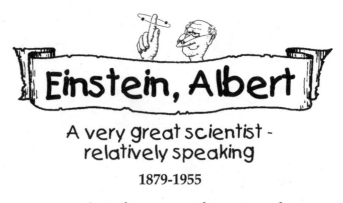

Einstein, Albert

A very great scientist - relatively speaking

1879-1955

Once upon a time there was ether everywhere, or so many scientists thought. The ether was a sort of nothing-stuff in which everything else existed. In fact you could almost say there was no such thing as nothing. Light was waves in the ether, gravity pulled you through it and if you moved through the ether it stayed where it was.

Albert Einstein was German-Jewish by birth. He wasn't very bright at school, in fact his teacher told him that he 'wouldn't amount to anything'. In 1901 he got a job in the Swiss Patent* Office in Geneva and became a Swiss citizen, and it was there that he did his greatest work. He worked in his spare time with nothing but a pen and paper to help him. As he was a *theoretical* scientist, he didn't need a big laboratory with lots of scientific equipment. In 1905 he published five scientific articles. All of them were amazing and one of them described his 'special theory of relativity'. It started a revolution in how we understand the universe.

First of all, wrote Einstein, let's suppose that light can travel through a totally empty space, that there's no ether for it to travel through. However, if there's no ether it also follows that nothing has any particular right to claim not to be moving or not moving. After all, if one object appears to be moving and another appears to be still, who's to say which one is doing the moving if there's no ether to compare them to? It's all relative. That's why his theory is called the 'theory of relativity'.

He then went on to show that pretty well everything else is relative as well, even mass itself is just another form of energy. The only thing that's fixed is the speed of light. He summed it all up in his famous equation $E=mc^2$, where E is energy, m is mass and c is the speed of light.

Even time itself is relative. In 1916, he came up with a universe in which space and time are part of the same thing, the 'space-time continuum'. A Universe where gravity is no longer a force pulling things together, as 67 **Newton** had thought, but is just a curve in the space-time continuum caused by mass.

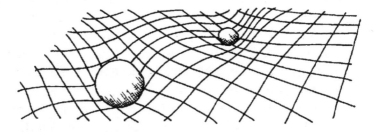

In Einstein's universe, when objects move (relatively) faster they appear to have a (relatively) larger mass and to get shorter, and at speeds close to the speed of light they become absolutely massive and extremely short. He also showed that time speeds up or slows down (relatively) depending on how fast you're going. Finally, and most dangerously, he showed that when mass changes into other forms of energy it produces so much energy that you can end up with an atom bomb or a nuclear power station. That's because in his famous equation $E = mc^2$, c, the speed of light, is such a large number that E has to be *huge* in order to be even bigger.

In his later years Einstein searched for a 'unified field theory' to explain both electro-magnetism and gravity, but he failed. Sickened by the growth of nuclear weapons he campaigned hard against them. By the time he died he was by far the most famous scientist since Isaac Newton.

Hahn, Otto

Man with a mission for nuclear fission
1879-1968

Otto Hahn is famous for splitting the nucleus or inner core or the uranium atom - for discovering uranium fission. During the 1930s he bombarded uranium, the heaviest of all elements*, with neutrons - tiny neutral particles. After bombardment, some of the uranium appeared to have changed into barium. Barium is far lighter than uranium, so how could this be? It must mean that the nuclei of some of the uranium had split in two. Hahn's result flew in the face of scientific thinking at the time and Hahn didn't believe the evidence of his eyes. It fell to his long-time friend, **Lise Meitner**, to reach the right answer.

211

When atoms are split a huge amount of energy is given off. This is what makes atom bombs so powerful. When the first two atomic bombs were exploded by the Americans at the end of World War II, at Hiroshima and Nagasaki, Hahn was so shocked that he thought of killing himself. Luckily he didn't. He went on to become president of the Kaiser Wilhelm Society in Berlin, now renamed the Max Planck Society for the Advancement of Science, where he'd carried out his most important research - and continued to campaign against nuclear weapons until the end of his life.

Fleming, Alexander

Scientist who discovered penicillin

1881-1955

Bacteria* are tiny micro-organisms. Some of them cause diseases. No problem - it's easy to get rid of them. Bleach, a flame-thrower or a tub of boiling water will all do the trick. Well, there *is* a problem actually - such methods tend to kill the patient as well as the bacteria.

What doctors need is something which kills disease-causing bacteria but leaves the patient alone.

Alexander Fleming was the son of a Scottish sheep farmer. Through luck and hard work he became a surgeon at St. Mary's Hospital, Paddington. One day in 1928, he noticed that a dish of bacteria which he'd left uncovered for a few days had started to go mouldy. This was nothing in itself, but Fleming noticed that there was a ring of dead bacteria around each speck of mould - the mould was producing a bacteria killer.

Fleming saw that the mould was *Penicillium Notatum*, a close relation to the mould that grows on stale bread, so he called the bacteria-killing substance 'penicillin'. Further research showed that it was harmless to animals and people. The flame throwers and the bleach could be thrown away. Penicillin was safe to become the world's first antibiotic. Fleming was no chemist and it took two other scientists, Florey and Chain, to find ways of producing it in quantity in the 1940s.

Geiger, Hans (Wilhelm)

German who recorded radioactivity

1882-1945

Radioactive materials give off, or 'radiate' highly energetic particles. The geiger counter is a device for counting the particles and thus for measuring radioactivity. It's basically a cylinder containing gas with a 'window' at one end. Particles of radiation enter through the window and create an electrical pulse within the gas which can then be amplified. The clicking sound of a geiger counter is the sound of particles being counted.

Hans Geiger designed an early version of the geiger counter in 1908 while working as assistant to **Ernest Rutherford** in Manchester but this version could only detect one type of radiation. In 1928 he and fellow German Walther Müller designed a more sensitive version which can detect most forms of radioactivity.

206

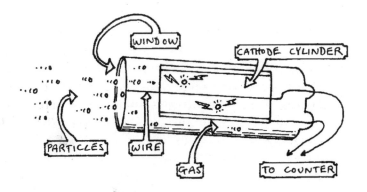

Bohr, Niels Henrik David

He made a quantum leap in our understanding of atoms

1885-1962

During the 1930s the storm clouds of World War II gathered over Europe. Niels Bohr was then director of the Copenhagen Institute of Theoretical Physics. His fame made him a magnet to young scientists from around the world. They gathered in Copenhagen where they were safe, and free to work together.

Bohr's fame came from his work on atoms before World War I. It was Bohr who proved that radiation energy is given off or taken in by atoms only when their electrons make a 'quantum' leap (sudden, total jump) from one level of orbit around the atomic nucleus to another. This was a big step forward in our understanding of the structure of atoms for which he won the Nobel Prize* in 1922. It also helped to prove the quantum theory first suggested by **Max Planck**.

When the Nazis invaded Denmark in 1940, Bohr, whose mother was Jewish, escaped with his family to Sweden in a fishing boat by night. In Sweden he worked tirelessly to help Jews escape the Nazi terror. He finally ended up in America, where he worked on the atom bomb. For the rest of his life he campaigned for the knowledge of atomic power to be shared between countries so that none would feel free to use it destructively.

199

Birdseye, Clarence

Pioneer of frozen food

1886-1956

In 1912 and 1916 Clarence Birdseye travelled to Labrador, Canada, as a fur trader. He noticed that the Labradorians would often keep food frozen over winter, ready to eat during the long, bleak winter months. This set him thinking.

Back in the United States he experimented with different ways of freezing food. He came up with a process for quick-freezing packages of food between two large, refrigerated metal plates. Although he wasn't the first person to freeze food artificially, this was the best method so far. At least some of the original flavour of vegetables, fruit and fish was saved. By 1924 he was ready to start producing frozen food in commercial quantities and founded the General Seafoods Company. In later life 'Captain' Birdseye became extremely wealthy, but he kept on inventing. His later inventions included a harpoon gun and a way of making paper from sugar cane.

Schrödinger, Erwin

He whipped up a wave

1887-1961

The problem with sub-atomic particles is that they're not really particles - at least, not all the time. Sometimes they behave like waves and not like particles at all. It was **Albert Einstein** who first pointed this out when he was discussing photons, particles of light. This indecision of particles as to what they really are, has caused a lot of problems for scientists. Erwin Schrödinger's idea of 'wave mechanics', published in 1926, makes the best of a bad job. It has helped scientists to work out the movements and positions of electrons inside atoms.

In Schrödinger's atom, the nucleus is surrounded by 'probability clouds'. They're not real clouds of course, in fact they're not real. But anyway, where the weather is worst, eg. where the clouds are thickest, that's where you're most *likely* to find an electron. In the present state of science nothing can tell you *exactly* where to find it, that seems to be impossible, but Shrödinger's equations are a lot better than nothing.

Schrödinger was an Austrian scientist working first in Vienna and then in Berlin. He hated Adolf Hitler and the Nazis and had to leave the country before the Second World War started. He only returned after the Nazis had been defeated.

Baird, John Logie

Pioneer of TV - watch this channel!

1888-1946

Baird was a Scottish electrical engineer. In 1918 he had to give up his job with the Clyde Valley Electrical Company due to the poor health which dogged him all his life. He marketed a patent* sock, then jam, then honey then soap. Each new business promised to be a success and each one failed due to his lousy health. He then had a nervous breakdown.

In 1922 he moved to Hastings. By this time people must have thought that he'd gone completely mad. He was determined to develop the first ever television. His first attempt was a crazy contraption: the lamp was mounted in a biscuit tin, the motor in a tea-chest, the scanning disc was cut from cardboard and the whole thing was stuck together with knitting needles, sealing wax and string. With this equipment, in 1924, he transmitted the world's first ever television image across several feet of his meagre, rented room. It was a picture of a maltese cross. He moved to London, still struggling against sickness and poverty, and in 1926 - success at last! He showed his mad contraption to fifty scientists - the first public showing of a television. By 1928 he'd transmitted pictures between London and New York.

221

Up until 1932, when the BBC took over, all television in England was provided by the Baird Television Development company. Ever inventive, Baird experimented with colour, big screens and stereoscopic effects until his death at fifty-eight.

Hubble, Edwin Powell

He gave us galaxies
1889-1953

Nebulae are vague, cloudy patches in the night sky, like milk stains on a pair of dark trousers. They're nothing much to look at without a very powerful telescope. Edwin Hubble started work at the Mount Wilson Observatory in California in 1919, which then had the largest telescope in the world. He saw that many nebulae are actually made up of vast numbers of individual stars. Among these stars he spotted several Cepheid Variables. Cepheids are a type of star which pulses with energy at regular intervals. It's possible to calculate the distance of a Cepheid Variable by the speed of its pulsation, and Hubble was thus able to calculate that many nebulae are far outside our own 'Milky Way' galaxy, which was then thought to make up most of the Universe.

We now know that there are literally *hundreds of billions* of 'extra-galactic nebulae' as Hubble called them, and most of them are galaxies in their own right. But Hubble went further. He showed that the galaxies are all moving away from each other - that the Universe is expanding. Hubble's law states that the *further away* a galaxy is, the *faster* it's moving away from the observer.

(The ratio of speed to distance is now known as Hubble's constant.) Galaxies at a distance of about thirteen billion light years* are receding from us at the speed of light. Beyond that distance we will never ever see anything of the universe because light given off by objects is travelling away from us faster than it can travel towards us. This distance is called the Hubble radius.

Hubble's work on galaxies and the e x p a n d i n g Universe leads naturally to the 'Big Bang' theory of the start of the Universe. After all, if the Universe is expanding it has to expand from something.

Sikorsky, Igor Ivan

He built the first working helicopter
1889-1972

Helicopters are terrifying if you stop to think about them. The entire safety of pilot and passengers depends on one moving joint at the centre of the blades. If that goes, there's no chance of gliding to land on the wings because there aren't any - you fall straight to earth. Igor Sikorsky always flew the first trial flight of his inventions, but the first helicopter flight (14 September 1939) must have been especially hair-raising. He landed safely.

Sikorsky was born in the Ukraine. His mother was interested in art. It was probably due to her that he saw the copy of **Leonardo da Vinci's** sketch of a helicopter, which started his interest in vertical flight. At twelve he built a toy helicopter powered by rubber bands and in 1909, having trained as an engineer, he tried to build a proper one, but had to give up due to design problems and lack of money. Influenced by **Wilbur Wright**, whom he met in France in 1908, he turned to fixed-wing flight and built a biplane instead (1910).

Then in 1918, the Russian Revolution broke out and Sikorsky emigrated to America. A few years later he opened his first factory in a barn. He manufactured flying boats (planes which land on water and widely used in the early years of flight) and the first aeroplanes with enclosed cabins. Eventually he sold his company to the United Aircraft Corporation and it was as part of the UAC that he developed the helicopter.

Shaw, Percy

Inventor of cats' eyes

1890-1976

Percy Shaw from Halifax liked a drink at Rose Linda's of Queensbury not far from town. Driving home in the dark one foggy night, he had to follow the tram lines because visibility was so poor. It was only the reflection of his headlights by a cat's eye that stopped him driving into the edge of the road. This set him thinking.

Shaw's cat's eye is a combined lens and mirror set in a rubber pad on a cast iron base buried in the surface of the road. The lens reflects car headlights back at the driver, showing them where to drive. When a car drives over the rubber eyelid, it closes, wiping dust from the lens.

Shaw patented* his invention and opened a factory in Boothtown, Halifax, to manufacture cats' eyes. It was built around the tree which he used to climb in his boyhood. Orders flooded in and Shaw became very rich. He bought a Rolls Royce but he still lived in his old house. It had four television sets in the lounge, but no carpets or curtains. He thought carpets were smelly, and curtains would shut out his view of the Yorkshire hills. He never married.

Banting, Frederick Grant

Doctor who stopped people dying of diabetes
1891-1941

The main symptom of diabetes is too much glucose (a type of sugar) in the blood and in severe cases, sweet urine caused by too much glucose in the urine. In normal people the glucose is used up producing energy, but in diabetics much of it doesn't get used at all. Chemicals which turn the glucose into energy in normal people are made in a body-organ called the pancreas, along with other digestive juices. Not so long ago people who had diabetes died a slow and certain death.

Frederick Banting, a Canadian doctor and World War I hero, worked out that groups of cells* in the pancreas, called, rather poetically, the Islets of Langerhans after the man who discovered them, are where the chemicals which digest glucose are produced. If he could isolate some islets he could extract the chemicals, the chemicals could then be given to diabetics and the diabetics would live. In 1921 that's exactly what he did, first of all taking the insulin from dogs. The chemical was called *insulin*, from the Latin for an 'islet'. Millions of diabetics have him to thank for their lives.

Banting received the Nobel Prize* for Medicine in 1923 - although he had to share it with a scientist called Macleod who'd done nothing apart from lend space in his laboratory. Banting was so angry he almost refused the prize.

Chadwick, James

He nobbled the neutron
1891-1974

Until Chadwick discovered the neutron, only two things smaller than an atom were known about. These were the two sub-atomic particles: the proton and the electron. Protons made up the nucleus at the centre of an atom and the little electrons zoomed round them. Electrons are tiny with a mass only 1,840th that of a proton and the protons are *massive* - relatively speaking. 99.9% of the mass of an atom is in its nucleus.

206
217 Chadwick, an English scientist, started his career under **Ernest Rutherford** in 1911. In 1913, he travelled to Germany to work with **Geiger**, but this was bad timing because World War I was about to start. He spent the war locked up in Germany. As soon as the war was over he returned to the safety of Cambridge and to Rutherford, to continue his work on sub-atomic particles.

It was in 1932 that he made his big discovery. He showed that about half the atomic nucleus isn't made up of protons at all - it's made up of neutrons. Neutrons have about the same mass as protons and are called neutrons because unlike protons they're neutral - they have no electric charge. Neutrons are useful for firing at other atoms so as to smash them up and start atomic chain reactions - useful for science, for atomic power - and for the atomic bomb.

Lemaître, Georges Edouard

Belgian who set off a Big Bang
1894-1966

Georges Lemaître served as an artillery officer in the Belgian army during World War I. It was this experience of war that started his interest in physics, and presumably in 'bangs'.

After the war he was ordained as a Roman Catholic priest but went on to study astrophysics - the structure of the stars. In the early 1920s, **Edwin Hubble** had proved that the Universe is expanding. It fell to Lemaître to suggest, in 1927, that, since it's expanding it must have expanded *from* something. To start with, he said everything in the Universe might have been crushed within an incredibly dense 'cosmic egg' which would have been about thirty times the size of the Sun. He pictured the Universe as exploding outwards from this 'cosmic egg' or 'primal atom' in a 'Big Bang'.

At the time there was a problem with Lemaître's theory. If Hubble's calculation of the size of the Universe was correct, and knowing the rate of its expansion, then the Big Bang must have happened only two billion years ago - and scientists knew that that wasn't long enough. Earth alone, was definitely older. It was only when Hubble's calculations were corrected, and the Universe was expanded still further so to speak, that Lemaître's theory became generally accepted. At present it's thought that the Big Bang happened over ten billion years ago and when it started the Universe was a lot smaller than a very smallpea.

Lysenko, Trofim Denisovich

Bad biologist of communist Russia

1898-1976

Trofim Lysenko was a biologist in communist Russia during the height of the Stalin dictatorship in the 1930s. Lysenko believed in the inheritance of acquired characteristics, as had been suggested by the brilliant 104 Frenchman, **Jean Lamarck**, more than a hundred years earlier. Lamarck's classic example of this theory was that of the giraffe's neck - growing longer from generation to generation due to its habit of browsing in trees. When Lamarck developed his theory it was a bold and honest attempt to explain evolution. When Lysenko dredged it 148 162 up again, long after **Charles Darwin** and **Gregor Mendel** had clearly shown that it was wrong, Lysenko was being both stupid - and dangerous.

He was Director of the Institute of Genetics*, of the Academy of Sciences of the communist USSR for twenty-five years (1940-1965). To curry favour with the Russian government he promised huge increases in crop yields and cleverly managed to make his wild scientific ideas fit in with communist preaching - eg. workers can grow into managers after careful education, so wheat can be made to produce seeds of rye after careful nourishment! The two things are completely different and this is not Lysenko's own example, but the fact is that he managed to blur the edges between politics and science. Several geneticists who opposed his ideas were secretly arrested and died. Russian biology almost came to a standstill.

Once the Russian leader Nikita Khruschev came to power in 1953, Lysenko's opponents were at last allowed to speak out. But it wasn't until 1965 that he was finally removed from his position as director of the Institute of Genetics.

Biro, Laszlo

Inventor of the biro

1900-85

Ballpoint pens have a small metal ball in their tip. This rolls freely in a little socket and is bathed in quick-drying ink from a reservoir in the handle of the pen so that the ink is rolled on to the paper rather than scratched on to it. Ballpoints were first invented in the late 1800s, however it was Laszlo Biro who developed the first really useful design. Biro, a Hungarian who lived in Argentina, patented* his design in 1938. It became so popular that nowadays all ballpoint pens tend to be called 'biros'.

Richter, Charles Francis

He scaled earthquakes

1900-85

The San Andreas fault cuts across California. It's where the land masses which carry America and the Pacific Ocean on their backs collide. And where continents collide, the result is either volcanoes or earthquakes or both. California has earthquakes - big ones.

Charles Richter was an American seismologist (a person who studies earthquakes) who worked in California. In 1935, together with fellow seismologist, Beno Gutenberg, he developed a scale for measuring the size of earthquakes.

The Richter scale, as it became known, was more useful to scientists than the older Mercalli scale. The Mercalli scale uses expressions like 'general panic' or 'many frightened and run outdoors' which mean a lot to the general public but aren't very useful to scientists, who prefer numbers. Using the most sensitive intruments then available, Richter and Gutenberg gave the number 0 to the weakest detectable earthquakes. Each number up the Richter scale meant a tenfold increase in size of earthquake over the number below. So an earthquake measuring Richter 2 is ten times bigger than one at Richter 1, and so on. The most powerful earthquake recorded since 1935 had a value of nine which, in old Mercalli speak, means 'damage nearly total'.

Heisenberg, Werner

He was uncertain on principle

1901-76

There have been several theories about what atoms look like. There's been the plum pudding theory, where the atom has a great big nucleus with electrons stuck into it like plums in a pudding. And there's been the planetary theory, in which the atomic nucleus is seen as a sun surrounded by electrons like planets in orbit.

Heisenberg shoved all such models in the rubbish bin. He said that we can never know what atoms look like. They're too small and too strange. We just have to rely on maths to describe them. In 1924 he invented 'matrix mechanics' which is a way of working out the positions of sub-atomic particles. Matrix mechanics are like the wave equations of **Schrödinger** - they tell you where particles are *likely* to be but they don't tell you *exactly* where. In some ways Heisenberg went further than Schrödinger. In 1927 he came up with the 'uncertainty principle'. This says that we can only be certain of the position and speed (to be accurate, the momentum) of a particle within strict limits. The more precisely we measure the one the less precisely we can know the other. The fact of us being there, measuring, means that we get in the way of finding an exact answer.

Heisenberg was a German scientist. Unlike most of the really clever German scientists of his day, such as Schrödinger, he stayed in Germany under the Nazis during the Second World War. He was imprisoned in England for six months after the war was over.

Carlson, Chester Floyd

He invented the photocopier

1906-68

The 1930s were a time of economic depression in America. Millions of men were out of work. Hoboes travelled the railroads, sleeping rough and taking whatever work they could find. During this period Chester Carlson lost his job in the patents* department of a large electronics company, where he'd been frustrated by the difficulty of copying documents at that time. He decided to work for himself and to invent and market a really useful copier. By 1937/8 he'd invented the Xerox photocopier, the world's first photocopier - *xerography* is Greek for 'dry writing'. Xerox copiers use static electricity to print ink from a drum on to the paper.

In 1947 rights to make and sell the copier were bought by a small New York company called the Haloid Company, which later changed its name to the Xerox Corporation. Chester Carlson died a wealthy man.

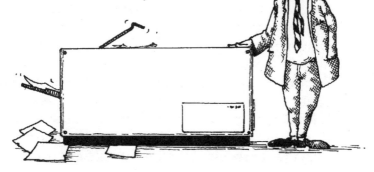

Whittle, Frank

He invented the jet engine
1906-96

Kick your heels in the swimming pool and you should move forward in the opposite direction. This is due to [67] **Isaac Newton's** third law of motion which states that for every action there must be an equal and opposite reaction. Equally, if you draw air into the front of an engine, compress it, and then inject fuel and set fire to it so that the air expands and rushes out of the back - the engine will move forward in reaction. This is the basic principle of the turbojet. It was first patented* by Frank Whittle from Coventry, a Royal Air Force Pilot, in 1930.

Whittle formed a company, Power Jets Ltd, with friends in 1936 and tested his first engine the next year. Unfortunately, the Germans were also experimenting and war was brewing. The first jet aeroplane took off over Germany in 1939 - not in England as Whittle would have liked, and it wasn't until 1941 that Whittle's design made its test flight. The superior speed and power of jet planes soon became clear. By the end of World War II Power Jets Ltd was so important to the British war effort that the British government took the company over. Towards the end of the War, British jet-powered Gloster Meteors were fighting it out with German jet-powered Messerschmit Me-262s for command of the skies. Whittle retired from the Air Force in 1948 with the rank of air commodore.

Libby, Willard Frank

American chemist who developed carbon dating

1908-80

Carbon dating is not two bits of carbon getting together for a candle-lit dinner. It's a way of finding the age of very old objects. This used to be a very difficult thing to do. Archaeologists look for clues in the objects they dig up: does this pot have a particular pattern on it? Has that stone axe been chipped in a particular way? Without carbon dating, their dates are sometimes little more than careful guesses.

Carbon-14 dating is completely different. It gives fairly precise dates for objects up to fifty thousand years old. The idea is the brainchild of Willard Libby, an American atomic scientist. In 1945 he was working at the Institute of Nuclear Studies of the University of Chicago and it was there that the idea occurred to him.

Carbon-14 is a radioactive material with a long half-life - it takes a long time for its atomic nucleus to decay, giving out radiation while it does so. Libby's stroke of genius was to realise that carbon-14 is being created all the time in the upper atmosphere when cosmic rays from the Sun bump into nitrogen atoms. So there's always fresh carbon-14 in the air. New carbon-14 is 'breathed' in by plants and thus also enters the food chain of animals. This means that all living things have some carbon-14 in their tissues. Not much - about one carbon-14 atom to a trillion stable carbon atoms - but enough.

Once an animal or plant dies, it stops absorbing new carbon-14. But the carbon-14 in its tissue goes on decaying and giving out radiation at a steady rate. All Libby had to do to tell the date at which something had died was to measure the radiation given off with a specially sensitive Geiger counter. He tested his idea by dating an historical object of a known date from Ancient Egypt and found that it worked. Archaeology has never been the same since.

Bardeen, John

The team which invented the transistor
1908-91

Electricity will pass along a semi-conductor - but not as easily as it does along a full blown conductor. You might think this makes a semi-conductor less useful, but that's the opposite of the truth. Semi-conductors have several remarkable properties, and they're what transistors are made of. Without transistors there would have been no computer revolution, no modern radios, televisions and other such devices.

John Bardeen, an American scientist, and his two co-workers William Shockley and Walter Brattain, started researching semi-conductors in 1945, at the Bell Telephone Laboratory in New Jersey. Their research led to the world's first transistor, which they invented in 1947.

The rest is history. In the 1950s, transistor radios became cheaply available and soon replaced earlier valve and crystal radios. Next came integrated circuits, where masses of tiny transistors are printed on to silicon chips. The digital revolution was under way, fueled at first by the need to cram as many electronic components as possible on to space satellites, and then by the vast demand for computers throughout the world. Silicon chips are at the heart of every computer.

Turing, Alan Mathison

Inventor of a computing machine

1912-54

Alan Turing proved that there will always be more problems than there are solutions. This sounds pessimistic but he only meant mathematical problems. He was a brilliant mathematician. He devised the *Turing*

Machine to demonstrate some of his theories. This imaginary machine was the foundation stone for the logical structure of later, digital computers. It had (or would have had if it had been real) memory, an input/output device and a central processing unit.

During World War II, Turing worked for the British government at their code-breaking centre at Bletchley Park in Buckinghamshire. He helped to crack the uncrackable German *Enigma* code and his ideas helped in the building of Colossus. Colossus was a very early electronic computer. This was before the days of transistors, so it ran on 1,500 vacuum tubes. It was destroyed at the end of the war.

After the war, Turing published his ideas on intelligence in machines and is commonly thought to have started the study of artificial intelligence. He committed suicide in 1954.

Braun, Wernher von

German rocket expert
1912-77

Wernher von Braun was the son of a German baron. He was hopeless at school until 1925 when he became interested in rockets and started working properly.

In 1930 he joined a group of rocket enthusiasts called the German Society for Space Travel. Next year Hitler

came to power and by 1933 the Society's research programme had been taken over by the German army. Von Braun became director of an army research unit and joined the Nazi party in 1940. By 1942 he'd developed the V2 rocket (stands for *Vergeltung 2*, meaning 'Vengeance' 2). In 1944, 4,300 V2s landed on London killing 2,511 people and wounding nearly 6,000 others.

After the War, von Braun and his team surrendered to the Americans. He became a US citizen in 1950 and by 1958 was working for NASA* (National Aeronautical Space Administration). He helped launch *Explorer 1*, the first American satellite and the giant Saturn rockets.

van Allen, James Alfred

Discoverer of the magnetosphere

1914-

Far out above the surface of the Earth hang two doughnut-shaped zones of high-energy particles. The lowest doughnut starts at 1,000 kilometres (620 miles) and the highest doughnut fades out at 25,000 kilometres (15,500 miles). The doughnut particles have enough energy to penetrate lead. Spaceships have to be protected from them or their instruments get damaged. Together they're known as the magnetosphere, because they're held in place by Earth's magnetic field - or as the 'Van Allen belts', after their discoverer.

At the end of World War, II James van Allen, an American scientist, was put in charge of a project to use captured German VII rockets, developed by von Braun, for research projects in outer space. The research included cosmic rays (high energy particles from outer space) which were a particular interest of van Allen. The rockets were useful but limited, so van Allen developed *rockoons*, rockets flown up in balloons before firing so as to avoid as much of the atmosphere as possible.

Then in 1957 the Russians launched Sputnik I and started the space race. The Americans had no idea that Russian science was so advanced and were desperate to catch up. Next year the Americans launched *Explorer I*. And on board was one of van Allen's experiments - a

Geiger counter to measure cosmic rays by counting high-energy particles in outer space. The counter went dead.

Van Allen realised that his counter might have gone dead because it had been bombarded by *too many* particles. By now the space race was in full swing - Explorers I, II III and IV were launched in quick succession. Explorer IV carried another of van Allen's Geiger counters, but this one was sheathed in lead to keep out some of the high-energy particles. This time there could be no doubt, and van Allen's discovery was proved in a final test when an atom bomb was exploded several hundred kilometres above the earth soon afterwards, disturbing the particles for further measurements. The doughnuts were for real.

Townes, Charles Hard

He made a maser
1915-

Electromagnetic waves are the greyhounds of the universe. They zip along faster than anything else. Gamma waves have the highest frequency and the shortest wavelengths of all electromagnetic waves, followed by light waves. Radio waves have the lowest frequencies and the longest wavelengths. Microwaves are in between radio waves and light waves.

Now radio waves can be produced artificially by an oscillating electric current (a current which changes direction backwards and forwards) as **Heinrich Hertz** showed in the 1880s. But the speed of oscillation of an electric current isn't fast enough to get microwaves started. In the early 1950s, it occurred to Charles Townes, a scientist at Columbia University that he could perhaps use the rapid vibrations of molecules to generate microwaves. The MASER (Microwave Amplification by Stimulated Emission of Radiation) followed in 1953.

Townes chose to work with ammonia molecules which vibrate at twenty-four billion times per second. By 'pumping' energy (either as heat or electricity) into a container full of ammonia gas he could force some of the ammonia molecules to radiate microwaves, at the same time that a weak beam of microwave energy was shining on them. This produced more microwaves which produced more microwaves and so on.

The MASER was the father of the LASER (Light Amplification by Stimulated Emission of Radiation), designed by **Harold Maiman** in 1955, which has revolutionised medicine and communications. On a more homely level: microwaves have frequencies similar to molecules, so if you beam them into a pork chop they make the pork chop molecules vibrate harder. In other words they make the pork chop grow warmer. That's how microwave ovens work.

Crick, Francis Harry Compton

Scientist who helped unravel DNA
1916-

When living cells* reproduce they pass on their 'characteristics' to their descendents. That's why worms are always long and wriggly, sunflowers always have yellow petals and you have two eyes and one nose. And why, although you may be wriggly, you're not wriggly like a worm, and you don't have yellow petals.

Information for all the characteristics (such as yellow petals) of a living thing are carried in the *nucleus*, what **Robert Brown** thought of as the 'little nut', which is at the centre of most living cells. The information is kept in a very long, thin molecule of a chemical called deoxyribonucleic acid - DNA for short. DNA is a long chain of all the chemical commands which make a living thing grow. Each new cell holds a chemical memory of the characteristics of its parent or parents.

126

The English scientist Francis Crick and his friend, the American James Watson, worked out that DNA molecules always come in two strands, zipped together in a double-helix (spiral) shape. If the strands are unzipped from each other, they form fresh copies of each other linked up in new double-spirals. Sometimes they unzip in order to join up with strands of DNA from a different living thing of the same species*, usually of the opposite sex. The new 'child' will then have characteristics from both its parents. And that's why you may have your father's nose and your mother's eyes, but you won't have yellow petals.

Franklin, Rosalind

Scientist who helped unravel DNA

1920-58

Every living cell* in your body has a giant molecule inside it. This molecule is so big that if unwound it would form a very thin thread more than a metre long - absolutely enormous by molecular standards. Its name is deoxyribonucleic acid - DNA for short. It carries the chemical code which tells your cells how to reproduce themselves so as to make you what you are - a human being with blond or black hair for instance.

DNA was first discovered in 1869 but it wasn't until 1943 that scientists knew for certain what it does. Then the race was on to discover exactly how it works and what it looks like. Rosalind Franklin was a brilliant English chemist. In the 1940s she had developed ways of studying the molecular structure of crystals using X-rays. She made important discoveries about coal.

Then in the early 1950s she turned her attention to DNA. She used X-rays to examine its structure. It had been suggested that the giant molecule was wound up inside the cell in the form of a spiral or 'helix'. In public Rosalind rubbished this idea, but in private she worked like mad to find out if it was true - for one of the forms of DNA anyway. She had already made the vital discovery that DNA can change between two forms now known as A and B.

Rosalind Franklin failed to discover the true structure of DNA. That fell to **Francis Crick** and James Watson. But she had helped them to make their breakthrough. Unfortunately she died at the young age of thirty-seven - four years before they were awarded the Nobel Prize*.

Maiman, Theodore Harold

He lit up a laser
1927-

Ordinary light is a jumble of electromagnetic radiation of different wavelengths going off in lots of different directions. Laser light, on the other hand, is all one wavelength and it all travels in the same direction. This makes it very powerful. A single, concentrated beam can cover huge distances, staying in a tight beam all the way, and then hit its target with energy levels similar to the temperature on the surface of the Sun.

It started with the MASER (Microwave Amplification by Stimulated Emission of Radiation) built by the American scientist **Charles Townes** in 1953. This was similar to a laser, but it produced a beam of microwaves. Townes realised that a similar device could be built to produce light waves instead of microwaves - a LASER. As things turned out, it was another American scientist, Theodore Maiman, who built the first LASER, in 1955. The core of Maiman's device was a cylinder of artificial ruby crystal. The ends of the ruby were polished and exactly parallel to each other. They were coated in reflective material, although one of these mirror ends was left semi-transparent. Maiman shone a powerful beam of white light into the sides of the ruby and this 'pumped' the chromium atoms in the ruby to higher than usual energy levels. As the energy of the atoms fell again they gave off photons (particles of light). These photons celebrated their freedom by rocketing back and forth between the mirrors at either end of the crystal. As they raced back and forth they stimulated other photons to match their wavelength, until a great gang of them, in the form of a laser beam, escaped through the semi-transparent mirror at one end.

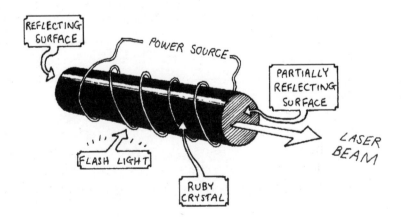

REFLECTING SURFACE

POWER SOURCE

PARTIALLY REFLECTING SURFACE

FLASH LIGHT

RUBY CRYSTAL

LASER BEAM

241

Bell Burnell, Jocelyn

She picked out a pulsar

1943-

In 1967, Jocelyn Bell began to scan the stars above Cambridge with a brand new radio telescope. She was just twenty-four years old. Her telescope was designed to follow quasars - 'quasi-stellar radio sources'. Quasars are thought to be the most distant objects in the Universe which we can detect from Earth. On reading through the results of a night's scan, she was surprised to find that her telescope had picked up a brand new radio signal from deep in space. It pulsed once every 1.337 seconds.

What could be making such a regular signal? Perhaps it was a communications beacon set up by aliens from outer space, which was beaming some sort of code towards Earth? For a while it was known as LGM - 'Little Green Men'. Unfortunately for science fiction enthusiasts, that turned out not to be the case. The source of the signal was a neutron star. Neutron stars are incredibly dense and small stars, perhaps only 16 kilometres (10 miles) in diameter. If they spin very fast they give off a pulsing radio signal. Which is how they get their name - pulsars. At the tender age of twenty-four, Jocelyn Bell (she changed her name to Bell Burnell when she got married) had discovered the first pulsar.

Glossary

BACTERIA (singular, *bacterium*): These are among the smallest and the most numerous of all living things. Each is made up of a single cell* (see **Robert Brown**, page 126) with no nucleus, and they reproduce by dividing. Depending on what type they are, bacteria can live almost anywhere: on the sides of volcanoes, deep under water - in other living creatures. Millions of them live on our skin and inside us. Around 200,000 per square centimetre live in the skin of your armpit alone. Some bacteria cause diseases and others are good for us.

CELLS: The word 'cell' comes from the Latin *cella*, meaning a storeroom. Cells are the building blocks of all living things, whether plant, animal, bacteria or fungus. All cells have an outer wall and an inner structure. Energy and nutrients are absorbed through the outer wall and waste products escape through it. Some tiny creatures, such as bacteria, are made up of only one cell each. Other living things are made up of trillions. The average adult human is made up of at least 100 trillion cells. Most cells are microscopically small but the largest single cell, the ostrich egg, can grow to 51 cm in diameter.

ELEMENTS: These are types of matter which cannot be broken down into anything else by chemical means. They range from the noble *metals* such as gold and silver, through *semi-metals* such as silicon and arsenic, to *non-metals* such as chlorine. Some are inert, which means they don't easily react with other elements to form *compounds*, others are very active and react easily with other elements.

GENETICS: This is the study of heredity, of how the parents of all living things pass on their characteristics, such as blue eyes or green leaves, to their offspring. Such characteristics are passed on in bits of chemical code, known as genes. In fact the word 'genetics' comes from the word 'gene'. All our genes are strung together in giant molecules called DNA (see **Francis Crick**, page 243) curled up inside each cell in our bodies.

INDEX OF FORBIDDEN BOOKS: A list of books drawn up by the Roman Catholic Church, which were thought to be spiritually dangerous. Roman Catholics weren't meant to read them without asking permission of a bishop. The first list was drawn up in the 1550s. The Index was abolished in 1966.

LIGHT YEARS: Distances in space are so large that they're often measured in light years - the distance light can travel in a year. One light year is equal to 9,460,530,000,000 kilometres (5,878,000,000,000 miles).

NOBEL PRIZE: The Nobel Prize was first awarded in 1901 and is based on **Alfred Nobel's** fortune (see page 172). It is thought to be one of the highest honours in the world. The prize winners for physics, chemistry, physiology or medicine, literature and economics are chosen each year by various Swedish academic institutions. The Peace Prize winner is chosen by a committee elected by the Swedish parliament.

PATENT: Inventors can apply for a 'patent' on their inventions. This gives them the sole right to make, use or sell their invention for a fixed number of years, often twenty, from the date of application, although of course they can sell the right to other people. The invention must be completely new, and the inventor must prove that it can do what he or she intended it to do - however barmy. Originally, 'patents' were written on 'letters patent' which meant, sealed with the Great Seal of England. Most countries give out their own versions of patents.

PRISM: A triangular piece of glass. When light enters glass it slows down. If it enters the glass at an angle this has the effect of bending it. The bending effect is increased if the light leaves through another side of the prism. Different colours of light bend differently and can thus be made to separate. This is how **Isaac Newton** (see page 67) was able to show that white light is made up of the colours of the rainbow.

ROYAL SOCIETY: The Royal Society of London for the Promotion of Natural Knowledge, to give it its full name, was granted a royal charter by

King Charles II in 1662. It grew from the Invisible College founded in 1645 by **Robert Boyle** (see page 62) among others. The Royal Society became the most important scientific society in Britain and is internationally famous.

SPECIES: A species is a group of living things which are closely related. Examples of species are dogs and apple trees. In higher forms of life, such as animals and plants, as opposed to single-celled creatures such as bacteria, members of a species can produce offspring together - and those offspring can produce further offspring in their turn. A Chihuahua can mate with a Great Dane and their puppies can grow up to have puppies which can have puppies, because dogs all belong to one species. Horses and donkeys, on the other hand, can mate together, but if they do mate, the female will give birth to a baby mule - and the mule will never be able to have baby mules of its own when it's grown up.

TRIGONOMETRY: Trigonometry is a branch of mathematics founded by **Hipparchus** (see page 24). It is a development of the theories of **Pythagoras** (see page 9). Known relationships between sides and angles of triangles are used to work out the unknown lengths of other sides and unknown angles.

Index

Published in 2014 by Wayland
Text and illustrations copyright Bob Fowke 2014

Wayland
33 Euston Road
London NW1 3BH

The rights of Bob Fowke to be identified as the author and illustrator of this work have been asserted by him in accordance with the Copyright, Designs and Patents Act, 1988.

Produced for Wayland by Bob Fowke & Co
Cover design: Lisa Peacock
Cover illustration: Miguel Francisco

A CIP catalogue record for this book is available from the British Library

ISBN 978 0 7502 8166 9

10 9 8 7 6 5 4 3 2 1

Printed and bound by Clays Ltd, St Ives plc

First published in 2000 by Hodder Children's Books

Wayland is a division of Hachette Children's Books, an Hachette company
www.hachette.co.uk